John Sheridan
with gratitude and
for your support and encouragement
during my 35 years membership
of Denham Golf Club.

Terry Bulloch

COASTAL ACE

COASTAL ACE

The biography of
Squadron Leader Terence Malcolm Bulloch,
DSO and Bar, DFC and Bar

TONY SPOONER

WILLIAM KIMBER · LONDON

First published in 1986 by
WILLIAM KIMBER & CO. LIMITED
100 Jermyn Street, London SW1Y 6EE

© Tony Spooner, 1986

ISBN 0-7183-0625-2

Photoset in North Wales by
Derek Doyle & Associates Mold, Clwyd
and printed in Great Britain by
The Garden City Press Limited
Letchworth, Hertfordshire SG6 1JS

To the brave young men, on both sides,
whose only graves are the Atlantic.
May such sacrifices never again be required.

Contents

Introduction 11

Acknowledgements 17

I   A Day to Remember 21

II   Early Days 54

III   A Setback 67

IV   Halcyon Days 71

V   A Score to Settle 85

VI   The Year of Survival, 1940 93

VII   Atlantic Ferry Pilot 102

VIII   120 Squadron 122

IX   The Bull has his Ups and Downs 151

X   In Another World 172

Epilogue 181

Appendix A:
German U-boats destroyed by Allied ships
and aircraft 187
Appendix B:
The Fate of *U-254* 189
Appendix C
Air Combat Report, 12th September 1940 195
Appendix D
Principal U-Boat Attacks by
Squadron Leader T.M. Bulloch 199
Appendix E
Sightings and Attacks on U-boats, 1941-2 201

Index 203

List of Illustrations

Opposite page

Squadron Leader Terence Malcolm Bulloch, DSO, DFC	32
Terry Bulloch's log-book entry for The Day to Remember	33
The corvette *Potentilla* reaches the scene	48
The next attack	48
Depth charges explode	49
The explosions subside	49
A half-term excursion from Mourne Grange (*Mrs Yvonne Boyd*)	64
Pipe Major, Empire Day, 1935	64
Campbell College, Belfast (*via Brian Wilson*)	65
Terry Bulloch at Campbell College (*via Brian Wilson*)	65
At Netheravon, 1937	80
Faithful Annies of 220 Squadron	80
A Flight, 220 Squadron	80
220 Squadron escorting the French President	81
C Flight of 206 Squadron	81
The Hudson	96
At Silloth, May 1940	96
En Route to Silloth	96
The B-17C Flying Fortress	97
The cockpit of the B-17C	97
Preparing to take off from Boise	112
Terry Bulloch in Hollywood	112
Flying Fortresses on Wright Field	113
At Gander, April 1941	113
On the *Tetela*, May 1941	113
Liberator I of 120 Squadron	128
With a Lib I of 120 Squadron	128
Liberator I	129
Sketch of the U-boat attack, 25th April 1942	129

Opposite page

Terry Bulloch with Liberator BZ/721   144
Terry's attack on *U-653*   144
The attack on 12th October 1942   144
A U-boat escapes   145
The sinking of *U-132*   160
Terry in flying gear   160
A Liberator waits for the train   161
With Wing Commander Charles Drapper of 86 Squadron   161
The crew that sank *U-514*   161
The Focke-Wulf Condor   (*Imperial War Museum*)   176
A typical Type VIIc U-boat   (*Imperial War Museum*)   176
With 120 Squadron after the Falkland Islands Campaign
                                         (*Crown Copyright*)   177
Presenting a South Atlantic medal after the Campaign
                                         (*Crown Copyright*)   177

A map of U-boat Operations against Convoys SC111 and HX217
will be found on page 37

Introduction

In the 1939-1945 war, the fate of Western Europe was decided by one battle. This was the Battle of the Atlantic, a five year struggle for the control of the sea-lanes to Britain. Winston Churchill affirms this, when our great wartime leader confessed that the only time he was afraid during the war was when it looked as if this battle would be lost. More positively he proclaimed, 'The Battle of the Atlantic was the dominating factor all through the war. Never for one moment could we forget that everything happening elsewhere, on land, at sea, or in the air, depended ultimately on its outcome.'*

If that battle had been lost, as it so nearly was, there could have been no question of regaining Europe. Without the constant flow of arms, food and equipment across the seas we, in our island, could not have survived. The millions of superbly armed Americans who later crossed the Atlantic to play such a significant part in the re-conquest of Europe would not have been able to reach our shores. The Allied victory of the Battle of the Atlantic made all things possible. If Britain had been isolated, Europe would have belonged to the winner of the titanic land battles being fought out on the plains of Russia, dominated by Stalin or Hitler.

Essentially the Battle of the Atlantic was between German and British forces. On the one side were the flotillas of deadly German submarines, their U-boats. On the other, British sailors and airmen. It is natural for Britons to think that a battle of this dimension fought over the immense spaces of the ocean which washes our western shores would have been won by the traditional guardian of our isles: by our premier service, the Royal Navy.

Yet it was not so. The part played by the Royal Navy was valuable beyond price. The battle could not have been won without surface

* The Second World War, Vol V

11

ships but, as this book will show, the force that turned the tide and which put paid to the enemy was the little known arm of the RAF – Coastal Command. Planes sank more U-boats than did ships. This is not to belittle the heroic work of the Allied navies nor of the merchant seamen whose resilience was beyond all praise. Until 1942, it was the Royal Navy that alone posed a serious threat to the U-boat enemy. It was also our surface ships that destroyed the German capital ships, such as the *Bismarck*. Yet the Battle of the Atlantic became a struggle between their ever growing number of U-boats and everything that we, in Britain, could throw against them. By 1942 the scene looked grim. Admiral Karl Doenitz, Flag Officer U-boats, the one German war leader whose influence never wavered throughout the war, was winning the battle. Month by month the number of U-boats in operation was increasing and so also were the numbers of our ships being sunk. With each ship sunk, we lost a precious war cargo.

For most of 1942 owing to a change of code by the enemy, the Naval Intelligence Centre at the Admiralty had been without the benefits of the vital information on U-boats gained through decrypts from Enigma, the German coding machine for top secret signals which was assumed by Doenitz to be impregnable. At the same time, our own naval signals based on outdated coding methods were being read with ease by B. Dienst, German naval intelligence. In 1943 the situation on both fronts was to be reversed but in the meantime the statistics of ships sunk were so terrifying that Churchill was only stating the obvious when expressing his anxiety.

During 1939 we lost 222 ships. By 1940 this had risen to 1059. Yet this ghastly total was even higher in 1941 – 1299 only to be exceeded in 1942. In that year our losses were double the rate of our ability to replace them with new ships. By the end of 1942 we were losing up to three-quarters of a million tons in a month. It was more than Britain could bear. Our losses in merchant seamen were especially irreplaceable. We were losing the war.

Yet the tide had begun to turn during the second half of 1942, although it was not yet noticeable – Admiral Doenitz, however, had correctly put his finger on the spot. In August 1942, he recorded: 'Successful operations were perfectly possible against convoys even when heavily protected by surface ships but only as long as Allied aircraft were not in evidence.' Later the same month, he wrote: 'Experience has shown that further pursuit [of a convoy] in an area under constant air patrol would be useless.'

This was followed by the order that, owing to the danger from the air, U-boats had to cross the Bay of Biscay submerged both by day and night. This was a serious restriction on their operation. On the surface a typical U-boat had a top speed of 17-18 knots and a maximum range of up to 6,500 miles. Underwater it was restricted to a maximum of 8 knots and a range of 80 miles.

Aircraft continued to turn the tide. By November 1943, Doenitz, now Grand Admiral of the whole Kriegsmarine, but still taking special interest in the U-boat war, was lamenting:

> The enemy hold all the trump cards ... detection methods against which we have no warning make convoy detours (away from U-boat packs) possible. The enemy air attacks have curtailed the mobility of U-boats and restricted our range of vision. They know our secrets and we know none of theirs ... The net result is that we have to give up the Western half of the Atlantic and restrict our attacks to the East of 35 degrees west.

In these pronouncements by Karl Doenitz (and there were others in the same vein), there is no indication that he feared the threats that Allied surface ships posed to his U-boats. In his mind, he considered that his fleet of U-boats could hold its own against surface attacks by ships. They would suffer losses but could hit back. But against attack from the air he was being made to eat his words. Earlier, in a rare boastful mood, he had declared that aircraft could no more attack submarines than could 'a crow attack a mole'.

At the end of May 1943 Doenitz had been forced to issue the most humiliating order of all. He ordered his huge fleet of U-boats to withdraw entirely from the North Atlantic shipping routes to an area west of the Azores. Not that the U-boat menace was over. Indeed during the months of April, May, June and July 1943, 122 days, exactly 122 U-boats were sunk; the bulk of these (87) were sunk by aircraft, mostly under Coastal Command control. There-after the pendulum swung dramatically. Allied shipping losses dropped to below their 1939 level and, some months, the Germans lost more U-boats than Allied ships were lost. American mass production of merchant ships was also underway and by year's end, the losses of the previous years had been made good. Europe had been saved.

The fruits of this great turn-around came in 1944 when the American forces were able to cross to Europe virtually unscathed. By mid-summer, they were in Europe along with their British allies. The great armada of ships that crossed the Channel on D-Day and the days that followed the initial reconquest of Europe, also crossed virtually without loss. Doenitz had concentrated a special group of about 40 U-boats in Biscay bases, within reach of the Normandy beaches, in order to stop our invasion at all costs. Yet every time that the U-boats attempted to attack, they themselves were first attacked: usually from the air.

This book is the story of the anti- U-boat warfare waged by Coastal Command, whose achievements in the past have been overshadowed by the more highly publicised exploits of Fighter and Bomber Commands. In particular, it is the story of its most distinguished, most decorated, most determined pilot, an Ulsterman, Squadron Leader T.M. (Terry) Bulloch. It was he who led the way and showed that U-boats could be attacked and sunk from the air. The example he set was soon to be followed. He also showed that the long range American-built Liberator (B-24), aircraft was the answer to Doenitz's U-boat menace and the successes he achieved with this plane enabled Coastal Command to obtain more of them.

It is surprising that the name of Terry Bulloch – 'the Bull of Coastal', as he was known, is not as familiar as those of the other great war aces of the RAF. In part, this is Terry's own fault as the book will show. Blunt outspokenness is not always appreciated. Happily the Bull is very much alive to-day and I am grateful to him for allowing me to tell his tale. It is also to my advantage, that I understand the dificulties that he had to overcome. For several years I also hunted the elusive U-boats over the grey waters of the Atlantic. I also served in Coastal Command. I also commanded a Liberator, and attacked U-boats. It was in 1943 that I first met the Bull at an RAF Coastal Command station in Northern Ireland and it has been my privilege to have known him ever since.

Churchill, with his mastery of language, wrote of the Battle of the Atlantic in these unforgettable terms: 'Amid the torrent of violent events, one anxiety reigned supreme ... dominating all our power to carry on the war, or even keep ourselves alive, lay our mastery of the ocean routes and the free approach and entry to our ports.'*

And it was Terry Bulloch, DSO and bar, DFC and bar, the supreme U-boat killer for Coastal Command, who had shown just what crows could do to moles.

* *The Second World War*, Vol III.

Acknowledgements

This book could not have been written without the generous assistance of a number of people, including the 'Coastal Ace' himself. Terry Bulloch's co-operation and friendliness have been invaluable. No biographer could wish for better assistance.

In addition, and at the considerable risk of unintentionally omitting a name that ought to be included; for which I apologise in advance, I wish to say 'thank you' to the following:

Terry Bulloch's twin sister, Yvonne Boyd, who, along with their childhood friend Howard Smith, supplied the information about the early days of Terence Malcolm Bulloch. My thanks also go to Tony Wilson for unearthing details of young Bulloch II during his years at Mourne Grange Preparatory School: this in spite of the handicap that the school has long ago ceased to exist. Yet John Carey added to these details: again my thanks.

For details of Terry Bulloch's progress at Campbell College, Belfast, I have to thank Brian Wilson, current Headmaster, and additionally the Rev David Erskine who knew Bulloch II at that College. The Headmaster has also supplied some rare photographs of those far off days.

Group Captain Tim Vickers has assisted with personal recollections of Terry Bulloch's early wartime experiences at Bircham Newton when both were operating Ansons. Jim Oughton, as well as offering photographs, also supplied a graphic account of Terry's record-breaking introduction to Trans-Atlantic Ferry flights during the very early days of that famous 'Atlantic Bridge'.

For good accounts of Squadron Leader Bulloch's outstanding accomplishments when operating Liberator aircraft of 120 Squadron, I am in debt to his former Commanding Officer, Wing Commander V.H.A. McBratney (now resident in Australia), to Peter Cundy – no mean ace in his own right, to Richard Wightman now living in the Bahamas, to Rae Walton, another whose dramatic story deserves a book on its own, to Norman Bristow and to Russell Laughton. Richard Wightman and Norman Bristow were also able to add comments about Terry's subsequent career, as a BOAC Captain.

I also had the good luck, thanks to the RAF Unit at Innsworth, Gloucester, to locate and interview two surviving key members of Terry's crew who flew a great number of sorties with the 'Coastal Ace' when serving 120 Squadron. J.R. (Jock) McColl was his ever loyal Flight Engineer and G.W. (Ginger) Turner was a WOP/AG described by Terry himself as 'the most efficient and reliable operator I ever flew with.'

Actually it was Jock who located Ginger for me although they had not met since the war. Together they were able to add colour to the bare bones of Terry's many attacks on U-boats, as supplied, in confirmation of Terry's own Log Books, by the Air Historical Branch of the MOD, thanks in great part to Group Captain T.C. Flanagan. The Air Historical Branch of MOD not only dug deeply into the Coastal Command Records but also supplied details of aircraft of those days. The Naval Historical Branch likewise assisted and, among other kindnesses, translated from the German extracts from the microfilms of actual U-boat Logs.

My thanks are also due to Mr Henry Hutson, an amateur historian with a great knowledge about the U-boats and their fates.

From Germany itself, I received assistance from Fritz Schmidt, a former U-boat crewman and from Otto Kretschmer, now a retired Admiral, who during the 1939-45 war was the greatest of all U-boat aces. I should also like to pay tribute to Lothar Gunther Buccheim whose book *The Boat* gave me a further insight of U-boat operations and of their living conditions. A quite different book which reminded me of various incidents and tactical changes made by Coastal Command during the Great Battle of the Atlantic is Alfred Price's masterly *Aircraft versus Submarine* (William Kimber 1973). Surely this must be the most authoritative book of these encounters?

For intimate details of the period when Terry Bulloch was experimenting with Rocket Projectiles attached to his Liberator, I have to thank Sandy Lewis. Sandy, a commissioned Air Gunner also gave me some colourful details of the period when Terry Bulloch was attached to 224, 59 and 86 Squadrons but, in effect, was operating as his own private Air Force – Bulloch's Own Air Corporation – the other 'BOAC' as it was dubbed.

Flight Engineer John Winston of the real BOAC has added considerably to the information I had about the post war career of Terry with that Corporation and has done so quite brilliantly. Thank you, John.

Last but by no means least, I must express my most sincere thanks to author David Beaty. David not only contributed personal recollections of Terry Bulloch when with BOAC but he unfailingly offered me sound professional advice: as did his wife Betty, another successful novelist. Without such encouragement, it is doubtful that this book could ever have been completed satisfactorily. David was but one of many persons who maintained that a book about Terry Bulloch was long overdue. He shares my belief that the name of Bulloch ought to be as well known as any pilot of the 1939-45 war in the air. My thanks must also go to my wife whose many accomplishments include the ability to rectify typewriters which, in my hands, tend to go maddeningly awry.

TONY SPOONER

CHAPTER ONE

A Day to Remember

8th December 1942

Convoy HX217 departed from Halifax, Nova Scotia, on almost the last day of November 1942. Its ships were loaded with food and war supplies for a Britain which alone was struggling to keep herself, and democracy, alive in Western Europe. The slightly slower convoy SC111 had departed a day or so earlier. Its cargoes were equally valuable to the Allies. Both were heading for Britain. Both had to run the gauntlet across an Atlantic Ocean infested with U-boats eager to kill. In total the two convoys comprised over 70 ships. The war in Europe was at a critical stage. The U-boat menace was at its peak. The absence of information from the decoders of Enigma was still total. The code had not yet been broken.

By 1 December the two convoys were running parallel barely 25 miles apart. Each occupied several square miles of sea. It was then that they were first sighted by one of Admiral Doenitz's U-boats. To the U-boat commander, the whole ocean must have seemed full of ships. Mastheads protruded above the horizon as far as the eye could see, like stricken trees after a forest fire. He made no attempt to attack. His job was to report and shadow.

At U-boat Command in Paris, Admiral Doenitz and his team, nearly all ex- U-boat commanders like himself, consulted the big charts which lined the walls of the HQ in the Avenue Maréchal Manoury. Admiral Doenitz was no braggart like Hermann Goering who ran the German airforce. He was a shrewd, calculating tactician, and was no lover of Britain. In the First World War, he had been captured by them when his submarine had been forced to surrender in the Adriatic. It still rankled.

The omens for a successful attack were good. In all, there were 22 U-boats strung out across the Atlantic within range for a co-ordinated attack. Because the convoy had been sighted so early in its passage, there would be ample time for them to gather themselves around the convoys and, like wolves, tear them apart. Not for nothing were his flotillas called 'Wolf Packs'. Another asset was that the weather was reported as being poor for flying. Realist that he was, he had come to fear attacks from the air, against which the U-boats had little to offer. The time of year was another good omen. His wolf packs had been trained to attack at night and in those Northern latitudes the December nights were long.

Further reports were received. A second U-boat joined the original shadower. The two convoys and their respective tracks were noted and plotted. The slower one was taking a more southerly track. Doenitz was never one to spread his forces thinly. The wolf packs were concentrated against the faster of the two: against HX 217 taking a northerly route to Britain along a track where the nights would be longer. Faster ships usually carried more valuable cargo.

On 2 December one of the shadowers was spotted by a Canadian aircraft and forced to dive. This meant that both sides now knew what to expect. Both could even predict where and when the attacks would most likely take place: in mid-Atlantic – in the so-called dreaded Gap; and in about a week hence. It would take that long for the slow lines of ships to reach the mid-Atlantic longitudes where the convoy would be furthest from friendly air cover. It would take that long for Doenitz, if he were to mount his most shattering attacks, to re-route his 22 U-boats from their various patrolling Atlantic stations.

The U-boats' tactics were well known. They had even been published in a paper written by Doenitz before the war. They were simple but seemingly almost impossible to counter. His various packs, each of about six U-boats, would be directed to the area where the enemy would be most vulnerable. By 1942, this meant the notorious Atlantic Gap far away from Allied airfields. They would be kept constantly informed by the shadowers of every change of speed and course of the convoy. U-boat Command would be directing all. Each significant report would be relayed to the wolf packs by wireless. When all were in position, the attacks would begin.

The report of the sighting by the Canadian plane prepared the contestants. German sailors, tired and weary from days or weeks at sea, would perk up. Diesel engines would be heard racing as the U-boats hurried to their rendezvous. Crash-dive drills would be practised. Torpedoes would be checked and greased. Navigators with compasses and dividers would be plotting fresh tracks. The time for waiting was over.

The British sailors could also guess what was afoot. Yet they would be almost powerless to thwart the enemy's purpose. The naval escorting ships were far too few in numbers. The Senior Naval Officer (SNO) responsible for guarding each convoy had a bare half dozen ships under his command. He could not spare them to desert the convoy, even temporarily, to search far and wide for any U-boats that might be shadowing his precious flock of merchantmen. A skilled U-boat commander could keep the convoy under surveillance from astern, on the beam or on either bow without fear of detection. He would see at once if an escort ship had been despatched his way. It would be relatively simple for the inconspicuous U-boat to escape detection from the much larger naval vessel. To ensure that no shadowing U-boat ever got within sighting range of a convoy required an outer screen of escorts far beyond what could be spared for the task. Another factor in the U-boat's favour was that several of the RN ships attached to each convoy were, of necessity, the hastily converted corvettes, originally designed as a whaler of such limited speed that a U-boat on the surface was faster than the searching vessel. The fox could outrun the hounds.

Even in daylight, hunting for a U-boat was like looking for the proverbial needle in a haystack. At night, it was impossible to detect visually a U-boat low down in the Atlantic rollers. It had been designed that way on purpose: sleek, dark and low with no great protruding conning tower like Allied submarines. It was little wider than a London bus.

British escort vessels found themselves in this predicament because the Government's defence policy, prior to the war, had been developed on a false premise. The Admiralty had assumed that enemy submarines would attempt to manoeuvre and attack from beneath the waves. To guard against this threat, they had developed an underwater echoing device code-named Asdic. Given good listening conditions, seldom available in the Atlantic, Asdic could detect an enemy underwater at sufficient range to render successful attack extremely unlikely. Pride in this invention had caused an official Admiralty spokesman to declare openly that Britain would never again be threatened by underwater craft – by the kind of submarine assault that so nearly brought her to her knees in World War I.

Few official statements have been so wide of their mark.

Doenitz, who knew about Asdic, found an almost fool-proof rebuttal. He trained his U-boat commanders to attack *on the surface* at night. As the evening light left the sky, U-boats would begin to close the convoy. In darkness they would move in to within torpedo range. Using what moonlight there was, they selected their targets and released their torpedoes; usually several at a time in a fan so that if one ship was missed, then another would be hit. With so many ships in the convoy, success was almost assured.

Almost the only drawback to this plan had been the high failure rate of the torpedoes used. By 1942, this deficiency had been rectified. HX217 was in mortal peril. The signs were that Doenitz would be able to achieve his biggest success of the war. It would be so great a triumph that, at last, he might be able to wring from the German dictator the priority of men and steel that had always been denied him. The ex-corporal Hitler was Army-minded and had little faith in the naval arm. Consequently the U-boat building programme, large as it was, never came near to the grandiose one that the ambitious Doenitz had since the 1930s consistently requested. By 1942, after the set-backs of the Russian winters of 1941 and 1942, Doenitz realised, even if Hitler did not, that the Reich's only chance of securing Western Europe, was to cut Britain from her suppliers across the Atlantic.

As the merchantmen ploughed their way through the Atlantic rollers, the Admiralty, well aware that the convoys had been detected, could do little but wait. Sudden alterations of course as night fell were one tactic that at times brought success. If the scent was lost, the U-boats might never again locate their quarry. In this case, the pursuers retained contact. Within days there were several of them as the ships nodded their way slowly eastwards.

By 1942 RAF/RN liaison had reached a high order. It had for long been noted that when a convoy was provided with air cover, its losses were few. U-boat commanders did not seem to mind fighting it out with naval ships. They won some battles, but lost a few. It was what had to be expected with the world at war. But they had a dread of aircraft.

Planes were always liable to catch U-boats on the surface unawares although the odds favoured the U-boat spotting the plane before the plane could pick up the outline of the U-boat.* The German sailors had excellent Zeiss binoculars and were rigorously trained to keep a sharp look-out: four men at a time stood watch in the U-boat conning-tower, each covering one quadrant of the sky. However, occasionally, the plane was the first to sight the enemy and an attack followed soon thereafter. At the start of the war, U-boats carried no anti-aircraft guns but as the menace from the sky became noticeable, Oerlikon guns in pairs had been added. Some U-boats carried several such combinations. A second tower or 'bandstand' had been added to carry these extra guns.

Fortunately for Britain, Churchill was a former First Lord of the Admiralty. Both he and the Chief of Naval Staff, the First Sea Lord Admiral Sir Dudley Pound, were of one mind about the U-boat threat and the role that the RAF, as well as the Navy, could play in countering it.

The arm of the RAF which was intended to co-ordinate with the Navy was a much neglected one. Prior to the outbreak of war Coastal Command was given neither the planes nor the training to counter the U-boat threat. Its role was to work with the big ships: to assist the RN deal with any capital ships that Germany might send to the North Sea. The latest planes were assigned to Fighter or Bomber Commands. Some called it the Cinderella Command.

At the outbreak of war Coastal's main 'strike' plane was the friendly Avro Anson. It was a slow lumbering machine with limited range and bomb load. In most respects it was inferior to its equivalent plane of World War I! It might just have been adequate for its role of keeping a watch for the German Fleet over the North

---

* Tests carried out in 1944, indicated that the odds were 3:1 in favour of the submarine.

Sea. It was totally inadequate for an anti-U-boat role over the vast expanse of the Atlantic. One squadron of the Short Sunderland four-engined flying boats had also been formed. This *was* capable of guarding convoys but subsequent production was almost stopped in favour of the ill-fated Short Stirling – a vulnerable and unsuccessful bomber. Also the Sunderland lacked the range to patrol far out into the mid-Atlantic to where, by 1942, the action had shifted.

Rush measures in 1940-41 had provided Coastal Command with several squadrons of American Hudsons. This hastily converted Lockheed airliner, aided by the transfer from Bomber Command of a few squadrons of obsolescent Wellington and Whitley bombers, meant that Coastal Command could, by 1942, provide limited cover for convoys within about 600 miles of the new airfields sited near the Atlantic. The acquisition of Iceland also helped, but this still left a huge mid-Atlantic area several hundred miles in width and depth bare of air cover. This was the Gap.

Help had come from an unexpected quarter. At the outbreak of the war in Europe, the USA possessed what it claimed as the greatest of all bombers ever built. This was the so-called Flying Fortress (B-17). It also possessed a secret bombsight with which, so the claim went, a skilled bomb-aimer could drop a bomb into a barrel from 30,000 feet! As a replacement for, or companion to, this super bomber (which could attain the then unprecedented height of 30,000 feet), a relatively unknown Californian firm, Consolidated Vultee, had designed an aircraft which claimed similar characteristics. This had been given the USA designation of B-24. Uncertain of its capabilities, a few prototypes had been ordered by the US forces for test purposes. The outstanding claim for the B-24 was its range: far beyond that of any military aircraft.

Although the B-24 was untried and had yet to be proven, the French Government, before their collapse in the face of the German blitzkrieg, had ordered a small batch. It was the only firm order that Consolidated Vultee had. When France surrendered, the British government, conscious of its unpreparedness to fight the Luftwaffe, took over all French orders for USA planes.

The Allied war strategy, after the Battle of Britain had saved the country from invasion, was to create a Bomber Command of such size that it could bomb Germany into submission. Bomber

Command therefore naturally laid claim to this windfall of the long-range bombers about to be delivered to France. For one thing, they could fly higher than any bombers on order for the RAF. Fortunately, the combined weight of Churchill and Dudley Pound prevented the B-24s from being seized by Bomber Command. The U-boat threat was never far from Churchill's astute mind and the First Sea Lord was honest enough to admit the Navy was in desperate need of assistance. Air cover in mid-Atlantic was what was needed most.

The French order (planes had to be paid for in cash) was a strictly limited one* and the number of B-24s was barely sufficient to equip one squadron. Moreover the planes had to be extensively modified for their new role: no longer a high flying bomber but a low level long-range escort aircraft. Not until late in 1941 was the squadron operational. They were allotted to only one squadron – the celebrated 120 Squadron.

With just a handful of these unique planes, now christened by the RAF 'Liberators', Coastal Command found it difficult to retain them or to keep them at their operational base, Nutts Corner, in Northern Ireland. Several were assigned as VIP Transports. One or two were apt to be whisked away for special jobs in Gibraltar or Middle East. Yet they rapidly acquired the reputation of being the aircraft most likely to detect U-boats in the far reaches of the Atlantic.

Perhaps the worst news of all for the RAF was that the Americans, even before they also became embroiled in the war, soon awoke to the fact that the B-24 was a winner. After the outbreak of the war in the Pacific, it became the plane that every US Service most desired. All this meant that over a year passed before Britain could obtain sufficient numbers to equip a second squadron. And then only by personal plea from Churchill to Roosevelt.

The Commanding Officer of 120 Squadron was a tough Irishman. Wing Commander V. McBratney soon licked the new unit

---

* The reason that France, with the enemy only across the Rhine, should have ordered these long-range planes, was that a far-seeing Frenchman had decided that oil supplies could be Germany's weakness. The B-24s had been ordered so that long-range raids could be made on Romanian oilfields; then the only ones in Europe and Germany's chief source of oil.

into shape. His Liberators were wanted everywhere at once. By the winter of 1942, they had been split into two main divisions. The bulk – a dozen or less – were kept at Nutts Corner but up to half a dozen had been sent to Iceland. These were put under the command of his most determined pilot. In charge of this small force was Squadron Leader Terry Bulloch.

*

The weather in winter in Iceland is generally vile: high winds, ice storms, rain, low cloud, fog and mist – everything that makes flying most difficult. The weather that first week of December was typical. The planes had to be kept in the open and it was a major task even to keep them serviceable. Terry Bulloch, who was never far from Ops Room and the Intelligence Office when not personally aloft – he was one of those commanders who made it a point to fly more than those whom he led, was following the progress of the convoys as they headed for their rendezvous with Fate. At the time, no one suspected how many U-boats lay in wait for HX217. The Naval Operational Intelligence Centre tracking room, although still without the benefit of Ultra, figured from its other sources of intelligence that up to 14 U-boats could be lurking ready to attack. This was bad enough. Only after the war did it become known that 22 were gathering.

By 7 December, convoy HX217 was just within range of the small detachment of 120 Squadron and two planes were sent to locate it and give it what protection they could. Only one managed to find the ships. This was not too surprising. The ships were still 800 miles from Reyjkavik, the Icelandic airfield. It was quite a navigational feat to intercept at such a range and in such vile flying conditions. The other plane suffered an engine defect and had to return to base. In spite of having had to fly so far, H of 120 Squadron was able to remain with the convoy for six hours. It saw no U-boats. This was not unusual. The U-boats generally saw their enemy first and took themselves down in haste as they had been taught to do.

The convoy was now deep in the Gap and the U-boats were massing for a grand slaughter. The night of 8 December would be their best chance. The weather reports indicated that the seas might have abated then. However one U-boat did jump the gun and near dawn on 7 December hit and sank a lone merchantman.

Meanwhile Terry Bulloch had been cooling his heels over in Ireland. He had taken off on the 6th on a wide anti-U-boat sweep and, as the weather had clamped down at Iceland, had been ordered to land back in Northern Ireland at Nutts Corner. During the 7th, he was hurrying back to Iceland. Back there, he weighed up the situation. He knew all about U-boats. During the past few months, he had tracked down far more than any other pilot in the RAF. His success had earned him the nickname of 'Hawkeyes' but to most he was simply 'the Bull'. It so neatly summed up his name and determination to kill as many Germans as possible. He had a personal score to settle and let nothing stand in the way of hunting down U-boats.

In the past months he and his carefully trained crew had tracked down no less than 19: far more than anyone else on the sea or in the air: more indeed than any of the other of the dozen or so coastal squadrons which made up Coastal Command's anti-U-boat force. Several, of course, had been able to dive to safety before the aircraft could be brought into an attacking position but the Bull had been able to drop depth-charges on about half of them and had inflicted damage on, or sunk, several. The pity was that the attacker could never tell what damage had been inflicted. 'WHOOMPH' would go the depth-charges, apparently slap into the swirl left behind by the U-boat as it crash-dived. Giant eruptions of water would be flung upwards as each exploded. Bits of wreckage and a spreading oil slick might mark the spot. Evidence of a kill? Unfortunately not. Perhaps only minor superficial damage. To destroy a U-boat with the depth-charges provided required almost incredible accuracy. They had to be dropped within 20 feet of the U-boat's main hull: always at a time when the U-boat would be both moving forward and diving; when the aircraft would be travelling at about 150 knots (about 250 feet per *second*) and would be drifting, one way or the other, across its heading due to the effect of the largely unknown wind speed and direction. Also the aircraft commander would only have an approximation of its height over the water and thus not know with any accuracy for how long the depth-charge would travel in the air before striking the water and detonating a few feet beneath the waves; provided always that the hydrostatic fuse correctly operated the firing pin in the prescribed manner.

No one knew better than the Bull that it was impossible to tell whether the U-boat had dived to the safety of its underwater refuge or whether it had taken its final plunge. In the former event it would be some time before it would dare to resurface. Consequently it would be pointless for the plane to hang about over the area in hope of a second sighting, even if able to mark the point of attack by a sea-marker. Also, of course, the U-boat would have hastened away from this point in some unknown direction using its electric underwater motors. Just occasionally a crippled U-boat might be able to force itself back to the surface by blowing all its tanks and there abandon ship. On those rare occasions its crew could be seen struggling into life-rafts and the kill could be visibly confirmed. But such a sight came to only one or two pilots throughout the war.

B for Beer, Liberator AM921, an aircraft which had returned with mechanical trouble the day before, was declared serviceable. Although he had been flying for large parts of the previous two days, Terry Bulloch had no hesitation in assigning himself the important task ahead. Convoy HX217 was in grave danger. The Bull invariably believed in leading from the front. He had developed a distaste for those squadron and flight commanders who kept to their offices and sent others to fly. Given half a chance he would fly virtually every day. His habit of flying more often than he would allow his junior captains to fly, did not win him any popularity stakes. He didn't care. He saw it as his job to find and sink U-boats and he knew that none could equal his record of doing so. The juniors' turns would come in time. A second Liberator was also serviceable. This he arranged to follow later so as to be over the threatened convoy at about the time when fuel exhaustion would require Terry himself to leave it. He selected his next most skilful pilot for this task. This was Squadron Leader Desmond Isted, commonly known as 'Wizz'. He, too, had acquired a reputation for finding U-boats in the featureless seas of the North Atlantic. 'Wizz' was only 21 years old and, like Terry, was destined to write his name in history in the days and nights which followed.

The Bull had trained his crew the hard way. He was a perfectionist and he expected non-stop optimum effort from all who flew with him. A key man in his crew was his tall good-looking navigator, a

Canadian, Michael Layton: at 28 the 'old man' of the crew.*

It was hellish difficult to find convoys so far from land. Only their approximate position was known: and that information was liable to be several hours old, or even days old. The Senior Naval Officer might have since decided upon a sharp alteration of course in the hope of deceiving his relentless shadowers. The weather around Iceland in winter is atrocious. 'A depression centred over Iceland' is a familiar expression to all who listen to UK weather forecasts. The convoy would be keeping wireless silence. Only in extreme emergency would it break this in order to 'home' an aircraft towards its position. The aircraft itself would never have an exact knowledge of its own position. Unknown winds would be blowing it marginally off track. The Met men did their best to provide information regarding expected wind strength and direction at the various heights that might be flown but they were handicapped by lack of positive information. Weather stations did not exist in mid-Atlantic. Ships kept wireless silence and, of course, satellite pictures were not even envisaged. Consequently, forecasts were little more than inspired guesswork.

Michael Layton had many talents and finding convoys was one of them. He was one of the few men whom the Bull trusted implicitly. Another key man in his crew was the No 1 ASV watch-keeper. ASV was an early form of air-borne radar. The initials stood for Air to Surface Vessel. George (Ginger) Turner was a taciturn Yorkshireman, and quite a genius at interpreting the confusing mass of flickering lines which appeared on the tiny screen (a cathode ray tube) of this new device. Sea returns from the big Atlantic rollers cluttered up the screen perpetually and masked the fractionally firmer tiny blips which indicated a ship or a U-boat (or even whales at times). Yet Ginger had developed an almost sixth sense of separating the one from the other. The device was new and regarded with such secrecy that there was scarcely any training for those whose task was to operate it. Also it was a crude early version and, having been hastily added to an already cramped aircraft interior, it had been uncomfortably placed in the passageway and was poorly

* The U-boat crews were equally young. The battle between them and the Coastal Command aircrews was essentially a battle between young men under the age of 30, yet the fate of western civilization was at issue.

screened against the light. Ginger was one of the three WOP/AGs on board. They had other tasks. They were also the wireless operators (WOPs) and the air gunners. They took it in turns to switch positions but when nearing an expected target or convoy, Terry Bulloch saw to it that Ginger would be positioned behind the tiny ASV screen with his head pressed against the hard rubber eyepiece.

Layton, Turner and the Bull's faithful flight-engineer, Jock McColl, formed the nucleus of this super efficient crew. When and if Terry discovered a man of exceptional talent, he managed to retain him as a crew member, no matter what others might think or decide. Another member of the crew was also a Canadian, the co-pilot, Pilot Officer Thomson. He had been with the forthright Ulsterman only a couple of months, but had already taken part in several U-boat attacks. An unusual difficulty which this crew had to overcome was to understand each other through the voice intercomm system which connected them via the earphones of their helmets. The Canadian accents of Layton and Thomson were unfamiliar to British ears. Terry had been born and brought up in Ulster and his voice retained elements of that distinctive brogue. Ginger's vowels were as flat as any Yorkshireman's could be and Jock McColl, a native of Kircudbright, had an accent that required to be cut with the proverbial knife. On the other two WOP/AGs, one was another Scot and the other just plain ordinary English!

True to form, Michael Layton located HX217 without delay. It was still dark with the dawn light beginning to spread over the eastern horizon. To find the convoy at once was a great asset. Precious hours could be wasted looking for it. On average, only about 80% of Coastal Command sorties located their quarry. Convoys moved as unobtrusively and stealthily as they could in order to evade their pursuers. At times these clever tactics also 'fooled' the aircraft which were flying to their aid. The Bull had been wise to assign himself to this particular flight. A less experienced crew might never have caught even a glimpse of HX217. The weather had been far from good.

'Hawkeyes' Bulloch knew precisely what the convoy's Senior Naval Officer would need of him. His job for the next few hours would be to hunt around the distant edges of the convoy and to try to locate and attack the shadowers that both he and the SNO knew

Squadron Leader Terence Malcolm Bulloch, DSO and bar, DFC and bar, as a BOAC captain after the war.

The page from Terry's logbook for 8th December, 1942, The Day to Remember.

would be there. The convoy was now in its most vulnerable position. U-boats from far and wide would have been summoned for the great killing that would take place that night. For more than a week the wolf packs had been gathering and preparing for the slaughter. Now that the convoy was in the middle of the Gap, the stage was set. This was the area where no serious threat from aircraft could be expected. The nearest airfield was some 700 miles away. Later, as the convoy drew nearer to the British airfields, the chances of being able to attack without air interference would steadily diminish. The night of 8th December could be the night of the long knives.

Keeping a dozen or so miles from the flanks of the long line of ships, the Liberator began its search. Ginger Turner positioned himself in front of the ASV screen. Hawkeyes, in his left-hand seat, ceaselessly scanned the horizon, his eyes travelling this way, then that. Thomson, seated abreast, kept similar watch on his starboard side.

Experience had taught Terry that most U-boats kept tabs on their quarry by trailing astern of the convoy. This is where he began his search. The plane was being bucketed around. He and his crew had already been up for most of the long night. It was as cold and draughty as it always was in those wartime planes devoid of heat and comfort. He was used to these hostile conditions. All the crew wore furlined boots, padded Sidcot suits, inner and outer gloves, scarves, helmets and as many sweaters etc as they could get into underneath. They made light of these difficulties. They had to do so. The Bull was indefatigable and expected his crew to be equally ever ready; ever alert. One advantage of the Lib was that its autopilot was, for the period, more reliable than most. This meant that the pilots were relatively free of the wearying task of manually controlling the plane; keeping it level and heading correctly. However while searching around a convoy, courses had constantly to be altered and each had to be meticulously plotted by the navigator on the charts that crowded his small desk. At all times Layton had to know where they were.

Terry's judgement was soon proved to be correct. Just before 11.30, astern of the convoy his exceptional eyesight once again brought results. Amidst the ever-changing pattern of white slashes that marked the wind-swept sea, he had spotted the fractionally firmer wake of a U-boat travelling on the surface. Not only had he picked up his twentieth U-boat but this time he had managed to do so as the plane fought its way through a hailstorm! It was travelling fast and closing up to HX217.

'*Action stations!*'

The crew knew what to do. The skipper himself would have snapped out the autopilot ('George' as it was called) and would be diving the big plane towards the target as fast as he dared. Yet it had to be a controlled dive. The only attacking weapons on board capable of sinking of a U-boat were the depth-charges carried in the plane's belly. They were weapons developed for the Navy and for use from ships. They had been crudely adapted for use from aircraft. They were little more than 'dustbins' filled with explosives (Torpex) and set to detonate beneath the waves at a preset depth. From naval vessels they were rolled over the stern or tossed over the sides. They were not designed for hitting the sea at high speeds, as from an aircraft. If dropped too fast they were liable to explode on contact or to break open. This latter was harmless to plane or U-boat but if exploding on impact they could destroy the plane dropping them. This was because Coastal Command pilots, in their efforts to achieve the desired accuracy, invariably attacked at the 'suicide' height of 50 feet. i.e. as low as they dared to descend. Another problem for the pilot in the few seconds allowed to him for the launching of a successful attack, was to position the plane so as to attack the U-boat more or less along its line of travel.

This tactic had been worked out by Terry Bulloch. It was almost diametrically at variance with the official tactic as decreed by the backroom boys in Coastal Command. These theorists had decided that the most lethal way to drop the depth-charges – at most the plane could carry ten, each weighing over 250 lbs, was to drop them in a stick *across* the U-boat's track. Terry Bulloch had been the first to point out that, in practice, due to the many unknown variables that had to be taken instantly into account, the chance of being able to drop the stick across the track was almost nil. Instead, he decided to attack *along* the enemy's track but at a slight (about 30 degree) angle to allow for the inescapable errors that could not be avoided. He had argued with his superiors about this, but remained adamant. Nothing ever made Terry waver an instant from his determination to destroy his enemy: certainly not any Top Brass in HQ who sat at their desks 1,000 miles away from where the action was.

The attack was the usual race against time. Somehow the plane had to reach the U-boat before it could escape under the waves. Without having to be told, the WOP/AG manning the wireless set would immediately begin to tap out in morse code the standard 'U-boat flash'. This was an immediate alert flashed back to base. Layton would rapidly prepare the plane's position in latitude and longitude and hand up the slip for addition to the transmission. At all costs, Command had to be advised that an attack was taking place. Tragically this was, at time, all that the Command ever did receive as quite a few Coastal Command planes never survived the next few seconds. It was rare for a U-boat to fight it out with the diving plane but, especially later in the war when some U-boats were armed to the teeth with anti-aircraft guns, such battles were quite frequent. At other times, the straining pilot would misjudge his dive and the big plane would catch the top of a huge roller or dig a wingtip into the sea as its pilot desperately tried to bank it into a low level turn. It was so rare for a pilot to catch a U-boat on the surface that when he did do so all caution was apt to be thrown into the wind. During the attack the bombdoors would be opened. They tended to creep back in the plane's slipstream. Jock McColl had solved this problem. As soon as he heard 'action stations' and saw the bombdoor opening, he would crawl along and physically hold them secure: although half hanging out of the plane. It was the kind of devoted service that Terry expected and received.

It was rare for a plane to see a U-boat first. All the odds were in favour of the four skilled watchmen aboard the surface craft. Against this was Hawkeyes' exceptional sight. Also the U-boats barely considered attack from the air in the Gap. This was supposed to be their happy hunting ground, far distant from any land or air base. No doubt, the hailstorm also played a part.

Too late, the U-boat Terry had spotted commenced its crash dive and it was tilting steeply as the Liberator swept overhead. The plane lacked any kind of bombsight. All depended upon the skipper's eyesight and split-second judgement. As a Coastal Command Commander-in-Chief commented later: 'Bulloch had a good bombing eye.'

On this particular sortie, the Lib carried eight depth-charges. Every petrol tank had been filled to the brim. On departure the plane was at, or over, its designed permissible weight. The Bull didn't bother about such niceties. He was a born pilot and in his hands, overweighted planes were no great problem. He swiftly decided that he would drop six of his eight depth-charges and gave the necessary order to the navigator who sat near the electrical panel controlling this. This modern timer, known curiously as the 'Mickey Mouse', also selected the stick spacing: normally approx 50 feet between each depth-charge. To elect to drop six and to leave two depth-charges unused was fairly normal. Although it was exceedingly rare for even a single U-boat to be sighted on a sortie, it had been known for two to be tracked down. Terry himself had done it once or twice already. One never knew when history might be repeated.

The attack was almost a copybook one. All six depth-charges were seen by the WOP/AG in the tail gun position, to explode one after the other in the prescribed manner and to explode around the U-boat just as it dived. Nos 3 and 4 apparently fell right alongside the fast disappearing grey hull as it slid under the waves with its stern protruding at an angle of about 30 degrees. Layton was also in a position to see well and with his usual precision had noted these details. If the hydrostatic fuses had triggered the firing pins at the pre-set depth (25 or 50 feet), then damage or destruction seemed assured. Almost at once there was visible evidence of this. A metal object, estimated by Layton to be of about six feet in length, came hurtling into the air and rose to a height of about 50 feet. Experts later conjectured that this was one of the U-boat's hydroplanes. Nor was that all. After this had settled back into the sea with a big splash, further eruptions came from below. These were quite separate from the depth-charge explosions. A great upheaval of water, dome-shaped, rose to several feet, followed by a rapid spread of dark brown oil. Later still, the crew aloft saw pieces of yellow planking float to the surface and, as if from nowhere, a large flock of gulls appeared wheeling around excitedly and diving down to feast upon something edible below.

The big clumsy RAF hand-held camera was put to use. Jock McColl had made it his business to use this whenever possible.

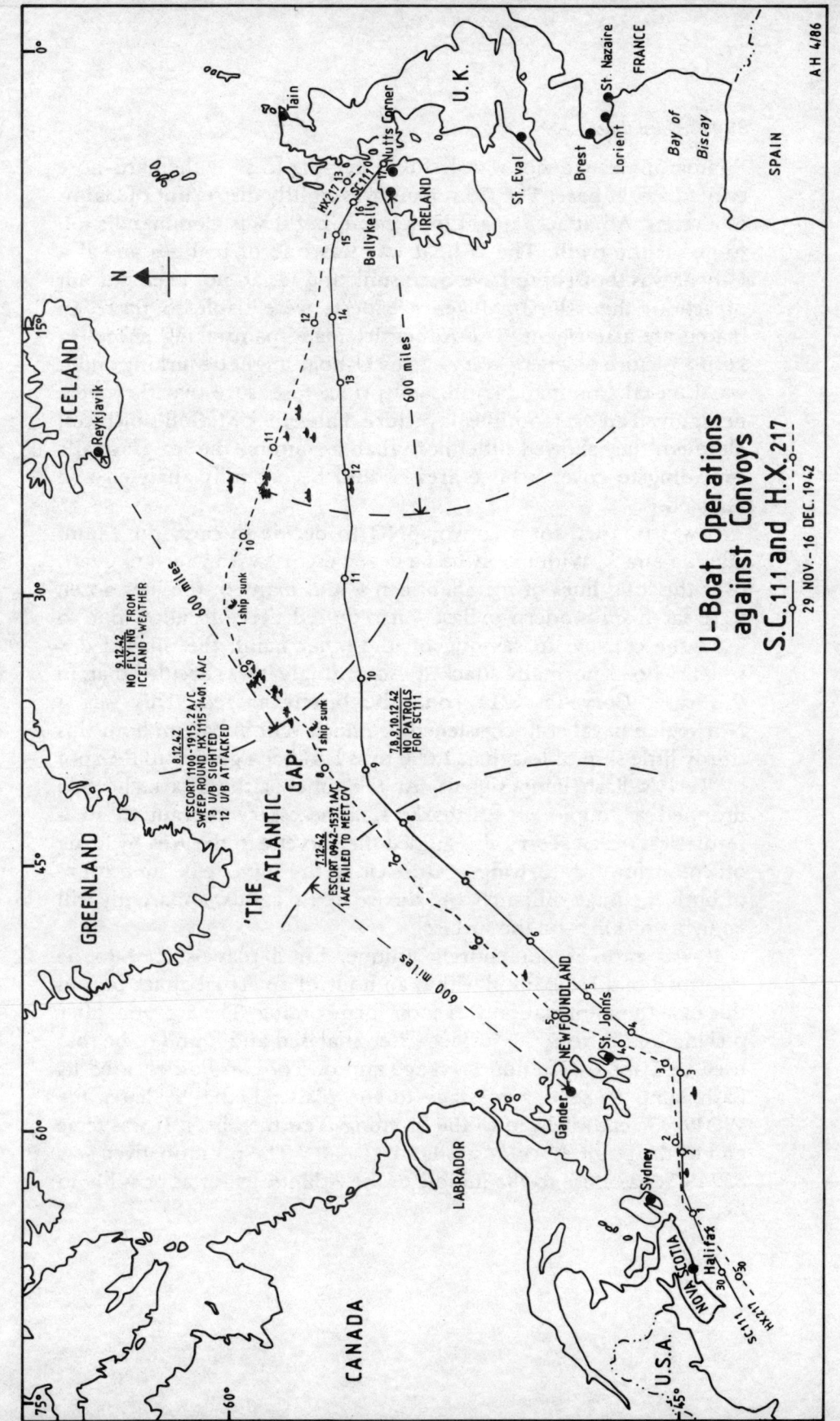

U-Boat Operations against Convoys
S.C. 111 and H.X. 217
29 NOV. – 16 DEC. 1942

AH 4/86

'THE ATLANTIC GAP'

7.12.42
ESCORT 0942-1531 1 A/C
1 A/C FAILED TO MEET CV

7,8,9,10.12.42
NO PATROLS
FOR SC111

8.12.42
ESCORT 1100-1915. 2 A/C
SWEEP ROUND HX 1115-1401. 1 A/C
13 U/B SIGHTED
12 U/B ATTACKED

9.12.42
NO FLYING FROM
ICELAND - WEATHER

1 ship sunk

1 ship sunk

600 miles

600 miles

600 miles

Reykjavik

ICELAND

GREENLAND

CANADA

LABRADOR

NEWFOUNDLAND

Gander

St. John's

Sydney

NOVA SCOTIA

Halifax

U.S.A.

HX217

SC111

U.K.

IRELAND

Tain

Nutts Corner

Stir

Ballykelly

St. Eval

Brest

Lorient

St. Nazaire

FRANCE

Bay of
Biscay

SPAIN

HX217 13

16

15

14

13

12

11

10

HX217 13

12

11

10

9

6

5

5

4

3.9

3

2

30

50

Photographic evidence was useful in helping to sway the hard-nose critics back at base. The Command was rightly distrustful of claims of aircrew. All attacks might look good, but it was Command's job to get at the truth. The U-boat war was one of realities and if a U-boat was thought to have been sunk and it had not been put out of action, then the Intelligence experts were liable to make an inaccurate assessment. The Admiralty made painstaking efforts to keep a picture of where every enemy U-boat might be lurking and it was Coastal Command's job, and pride, to ensure that they were never given an over-optimistic picture. Later Jock McColl's pictures, although they showed little more than a stain on the sea gradually spreading to cover a huge area, would be carefully analysed and assessed.

It was unusual for a convoy SNO to decide to carry on a hunt after an attack. With barely half a dozen escorts with which to guard over the long lines of merchantmen – and many of the half dozen were far from modern or fast – it required nerve to allow one to leave the convoy. It was not, on the other hand, the time of day when U-boats normally attacked. Accordingly it was decided that, in this case, Corvette K214 could be briefly spared. This was a Norwegian naval craft christened *Potentilla*. Within half an hour this sturdy little ship of less than 1,000 tons had been guided to the spot by Terry's flash lamp signals. At the time of the attack, he had dropped a couple of sea-markers, a necessary precaution in a featureless ocean. Terry also guided the corvette to the area by firing off colourful Very cartridges. Once close, the corvette became aware of both the huge oil patch and the excited seagulls, apparently still enjoying pickings on the surface.

It was rare, if not entirely unique, for a plane's crew to be informed of a U-boat kill within an hour of an actual attack but, in this case the information was soon forthcoming. The corvette, after picking up oil from the surface (later analysed and found to be that used by U-boats), minor wreckage and one or two bodies, used its flash lamp to send a message to the plane. Letter by letter the WOP/AG read it aloud to the listening crew members. It was terse and to the point. 'Y-O-U K-I-L-L-E-D H-I-M!!' The position given was 35° 19'W; as close to the middle of the Atlantic as it was possible to be.

Although it is in Coastal Command's official records that this attack accounted for *U-254* and although there is not the slightest doubt that *U-254* never survived this particular day, a postwar story, believed by some who have investigated U-boat kills, tells a strange, quite different, tale. Postwar German accounts reveal yet another quite different story. The accounts are so confusing and contradictory that the matter is dealt with separately in an appendix to this book. Events that happened in mid-Atlantic 40 years ago are difficult to reconstruct. U-boat kills were at best almost impossible to confirm at the time unless survivors could be picked up. Seldom was this so. Most U-boats sunk by underwater detonation of depth-charges went down and kept on going down. Once their hulls were ruptured, they rapidly filled with water and no amount of blowing of tanks could aid them. Several hundred must still lie on the ocean floor, each with their crew of 44 or more, still with them.

The elation of the Bull and his crew of the news from the *Potentilla* can only be imagined. After so many tedious hours of flying: after so many other promising attacks on other U-boats, to receive such a message from a surface ship in such positive terms was a unique and wonderful experience. It made the incessant cold and ever present bumpiness of flying beneath the low cloud of the Atlantic, the grim metal interior of the plane, the almost incredibly long hours of each flight, all seem as nothing. They had accomplished what they had been trained to do. They had killed a U-boat. The corvette had told them so.

But there were other things to do. The patrol had to be maintained. The procedure also called for details of the attack to be transmitted back to base. For security reasons, these had to be sent in code. The procedures and the coding machine were complicated. It took time to send even simple messages and the reception conditions were poor. Many messages had to be repeated. Even in wartime, the Services required important details to be logged – and done so in an official manner beset with red tape.

Barely had the details been duly logged when: *Action stations!* Once again the Bull had spied another U-boat. The telltale signs in the water told him that this time he had picked up *two* U-boats travelling together about 300 yards apart at a distance of about 20 miles from the convoy and 'going like mad', as the Bull said, 'to catch up'. The U-boats were on the aircraft's port bow. The nearer had been quick to spot the Lib and was hastily crash-diving. The other, which appeared to be trailing oil, was less alert but managed to submerge as the Bull in B/120 came roaring overhead. It had only submerged for about 15 seconds. This meant that there was still a chance of inflicting damage or of scoring a second kill. The two remaining depth-charges had been armed and selected in the few seconds available. The crew knew their drills. With the Bull in charge, they knew that they had to be on the top line at all times or else ... The Bull's wrath would be blistering if a false move had been made. He could be as unmerciful of inefficiency with his crew as he could be with the sworn enemy. He neither asked nor gave quarter. The Britain he loved was at war: war with no holds barred. It was them or us; a fight to the finish.

The two depth-charges were dropped about 200 feet ahead of the swirl left behind by the diving U-boat. Both were seen to explode just above where the conning tower was likely to have been. After the spray subsided there was a further upheaval about 50 feet ahead of the earlier explosions. It rose to about 30 feet: solid water not just spray. In the rear-gunner's estimation, it was considerably larger than any air bubble rising to the surface as a result of a U-boat blowing its tanks to achieve stability underwater. It indicated damage below. It took a minute or more to haul the large plane around and back to the area and, by the time that Terry could see for himself, there was nothing beyond the usual residue of swirl marks. It was 12.45, barely 75 minutes after the first attack. This was turning out to be quite a day for the Ulsterman and his crew.

Once again the follow-up procedures were carried out. The feelings on board were less euphoric. The crew were in their more customary position of doubt. Had they sent another U-boat to the bottom? How could they tell? It was maddening not to know. A ship hunting a U-boat generally knew one way or another, with some certainty. It could remain in the area for hours on end. It had underwater listening devices. It could scour the area for tell-tale evidence, as *Potentilla* had done, and pick up pieces for subsequent evaluation. Occasionally it picked up bodies. It also knew when an enemy had got away, as was so often the case. A ship carried large numbers of depth-charges. It could drop stick after stick. Unlike the plane, it could alter the depth-setting fuses.

Naval vessels also carried guns in case the enemy resurfaced: they also carried torpedoes. Moreover they could, and did, ram U-boats on the surface with deadly effect. By contrast a plane had to kill or miss during one swift run: one bare half-chance to discharge its small load of depth-charges, all pre-set to detonate at the same shallow depth. That one hasty run had to be exactly right.

Although the crew of the plane obtained little satisfaction from the inconclusive attack, the effect below was considerable. Even if undamaged, a U-boat forced to crash-dive had problems. Once below, it really was as blind as a mole. Had it been reported? Would surface ships be hurrying to its vulnerable position? For how long should it remain below? The longer it stayed out of sight, the less was its chance of being attacked again from the air. It never seems to have been appreciated by U-boat commanders that planes were liable to unload all, or nearly all, their depth-charges on their first run. Yet, when in pursuit of a convoy, the longer it stayed submerged, the less was the chance of its being able to regain contact with the enemy. It was left totally in the dark to guess what might be happening overhead. Fears tend to multiply under such conditions. It was quite likely that the particular U-boat crew had never before been surprised and attacked from the air. Henceforth, it would be a more prudent and more fearful crew. Admiral Doenitz knew only too well, and had publicly said so, that an underwater force had to be offensive-minded. Once it began to think defensively, its effectiveness was greatly diminished. It was never difficult for a U-boat to keep out of sight and to avoid being attacked. It required excessive nerve and courage to enter the fray.

Although the attack had been inconclusive, all aboard knew that they had made history. Most crews flew for months or years before sighting a U-boat* yet, although they had only been around the convoy for less than two hours, they had sighted three and attacked two. They also knew that their captain, truly Hawkeyes, had now sighted 22 and attacked 12: far more than most *squadrons* had, or

---

* The author sighted his first U-boat on his 92nd operational trip over water. Over 50 of these had been specific anti-U-boat sorties.

ever did, throughout five years of war over the Atlantic. Squadron Leader Terry Bulloch was fast becoming a living legend.

Terry Bulloch and his crew still faced many hours of cold, bumpiness and watchfulness before they could turn for 'home', some 700 miles away. Their ability to stay in the air so long was partially due to Jock McColl's skilful manipulation of the aircraft's fuel supply. Working closely with his captain, Jock had devised a number of ways of conserving fuel. Each sortie, especially the convoy-guarding ones, required two quite separate techniques. When proceeding towards the convoy, and also when returning from one, maximum fuel economy meant maximum miles per gallon. The navigator came into this calculation, too. Generally, a good economy could be achieved by flying at about 5,000 feet. But, as the winds at the various levels would affect the flight – either aiding groundspeed or detracting from it, Layton had to calculate how best to proceed. After that Terry and Jock would apply all the tricks they had learnt. Unlike most British aircraft engines of that time, the USA Pratt & Whitney motors of the Lib had manual, rather than automatic, fuel control units. They could be leaned off. However, if flown too lean, they were apt to backfire and the engine would be damaged. Much was determined by 'feel' and vibration. There were no scientific charts to advise the crew. Even the exhaust gases were studied. At night the tail pipes of the engines would glow red as the exhaust gases escaped. Red meant that some fuel was not being consumed. By leaning off, the gases would become almost colourless. If blue, then the chances were that the engines were running too lean.

Over the convoy, a quite different technique was required. Miles were of little consequence. The trick was to be able to stay close to the ships for as long as possible. Normally, an aircraft flying at a slow speed is not operating efficiently but around the convoy this hardly mattered. Consequently, when on guard over the ships, the throttles would be pulled back and an economical loiter flight pattern would be set up. By such careful attention to details, a skilful dedicated captain could extend the flight time by as much as two hours. A 15-hour sortie could be turned into a 17-hour one. While two hours additional to 15 was not a great improvement, it became of considerable significance in those instances, such as all convoy protection flights, when several hours had to be spent getting to, and returning from, the area where U-boats were most likely to be located. Vigilance at the fuel panel was almost as important as vigilance at the look-out stations. As the Bull said afterwards in an interview: 'The crew are as keen as mustard.' This was no surprise as they had become the most successful aircrew ever to hunt down U-boats. They also knew that their captain would not have hesitated to have dismissed them if not up to his standards. Already in Iceland, he had sent back an experienced captain because, in his opinion, he had failed to maintain the high standard required.

The fact that the Lib now had no depth-charges did not alter the role that it had to play. The U-boat commander could not possibly know that an aircraft diving at him had no means of sinking him.* The depth-charges were stowed internally and no sane U-boat commander was going to await until the bomb doors of the plane opened to see whether they were empty or not!

One asset of operating out of Iceland was that food there was not rationed as it was in the UK. It was true that the island lacked vegetables as it contained very little topsoil but since being (forcibly) taken over by the Americans and British, meat seemed almost inexhaustible. Steaks, virtually unheard of in Britain for years, were there in plenty and Terry had arranged to get hold of some and to have found a way of serving them hot on board. Already they had been on patrol for hours and all had been exceptionally busy. It was time to get stuck into the steaks.

The Bull, as usual, ate with his plate on his lap. Never for more than a second or two would he take his eyes away from the grey waters below. As he ate, he continued to scan: this way and that.

'*Action stations!*'

He had spotted yet another U-boat. Plates and food went crashing to the floor as the crew jumped to their assigned positions.

The Bull was quite fearless. For all he knew, this U-boat might decide to fight back. He had no depth-charges. No matter. He swung the plane into a tight turn and dived down. No need to dive

---

* Early in the war, because no fighting planes were available for anti-U-boat patrols, unarmed planes, even Tiger Moth training bi-planes, had been sent on patrol over the North Sea to frighten away U-boats. These were known as Scarecrow patrols.

with care this time. There could be no chance of depth-charges exploding prematurely. His Lib had been fitted with 4×20mm cannons fixed to fire forwards in the nose. Originally the belief was that these could cripple U-boats. It was not until a U-boat was captured intact in 1941 that it was realised how sturdily they had been constructed; with plates both riveted and welded and almost 1 whole inch of steel thick. The 20mm cannon shells would never penetrate such hulls. Only if a U-boat fought it out with the diving Lib could the cannons play a decisive role. They could certainly blow a few heads off in a crowded conning tower.

True to expectations, U-boat No 4 of this patrol began the frenzied race to get below before it could be attacked from above. The cannons were fed from clips. Each held 15 rounds; 60 rounds in all. There was no means of aiming other than to point the aircraft's nose at the target. All 60 were released in one furious burst and several appeared to hit around the already deserted conning tower. If they did so, they would have certainly have sounded almost lethal to the men in the diving vessel. Perhaps another minor dent in a crew's morale?

After such an attack, the immediate action was to send a man below to re-arm the guns with replacement clips. The Bull could not claim even minor damage but he had done his best. The most positive evidence of damage was the remains of the steak and chips littering the aircraft floor! As the skipper commented later: 'Our lunch was ruined but that sub didn't get within torpedo range of the convoy.'

Scarcely had the guns been reloaded, the incident duly logged timed at 1426 and the required reports sent to base, when yet another U-boat was spotted. The sea seemed to be full of them: as indeed it was. In a later press interview the Bull said: 'Subs kept bobbing up all over the place. We'd no sooner finished one attack and got all the details logged when another would show up.' Doenitz had summoned them from far and wide. This was a prize convoy. Given luck with the weather, he hoped to rub it out completely. Recently, over twenty ships had been lost from one convoy and November 1942 had been the record month for tonnage sunk – over three quarters of a million. Perhaps December's total would exceed this? Britain would be starved into submission or, at least, rendered impotent. It seemed a very real possibility. A stupendous success at sea at this critical moment of the war, might swing the balance in Germany's favour: might cancel out the Russian reverses?

Again the captain sent the plane into a flat-out dive. It reminded him of near suicide attacks he had made in Hudsons two years earlier when Britain stood in such grave peril of invasion from across the Channel. His targets then had been the ports from which the invasion seemed about to be launched. They had been filled with invasion barges and Terry and others from Coastal Command had been ordered to risk all to attack them. Many had been shot down and killed but he had survived. 120 Squadron contained others who had survived. It was a hand-picked unit. Coastal Command didn't intend to let just anyone fly their few precious long-range Liberators. Only the best.

Again, all that Bf120 could possibly achieve would be to fire off his 60 rounds, shake up the enemy and so to make him lose contact with the quarry which for days had been the sole purpose of the long chase. It was now nearly three o'clock on the squally December day. Time enough to regain contact and to be able to catch up for a night attack would be running out for the pursuing wolf packs. If the SNO made an abrupt change of track* as night fell, the chances were that only those U-boats in immediate contact would be able to follow the move. The odds were against U-boat No 5 again catching up with HX217.

No 6 was spotted at 1524 while the crew were warming themselves with mugs of hot tea from the thermos flasks they carried. The cannons had again been replenished and again were fired as the Bull dived. This U-boat also did not linger to find out if the attacking Lib carried depth-charges. Like the others, its commander was probably astonished to be attacked from the air when in a supposedly 'plane-free' area. In the plane the crew could scarcely believe what they were seeing. Almost on the hour and at every hour, they were hearing their captain yell, *'Action stations'*. It was becoming a routine and down would go the plane into a lurching dive with guns blazing.

---

* So great were some of these abrupt changes that some convoys almost went round in a circle.

Scarcely anyone in 120 Squadron had ever fired those guns before. Now they had only four more clips of ammunition left.

It was equally unreal to the enemy below. To them, the sky must have seemed full of huge diving planes. But how had they got there? These four-engined attackers were not the kind that aircraft carriers ever disgorged. Had their compasses all gone awry? Were they really 700 miles or more from the nearest land? Had they travelled all that way at fast speed (burning up fuel reserves) only to run into a point in mid-Atlantic which appeared to be rendezvous for half the RAF? Were they going to be denied a chance to attack the fat convoy which they had been stalking for so long?

It was heartening for the crew above to see the enemy scuttling below the waves but it was disappointing that they had no depth-charges to sling into the diving swirl below. All possible records had been broken. It was unbelievable. They had put down *six* U-boats: roughly one for each of the hours they had spent hunting around the convoy's flanks. It was heartening, too, for the harried merchant seamen below. The old hands had been sunk once or twice before. They knew, even if the keen youngsters around them did not, that their ship was in the critical point of their dangerous passage. By 1942, most ships' crews had ceased to shoot furiously at every plane that they saw. During 1939-41 this had been the tactic: and rightly so since the German long-range Condors were initially the planes that they were most likely to encounter over the Atlantic and these had proved themselves very capable of bombing and sinking ships. A few ships' crews still 'shot first and asked questions later' but most now watched for the recognition 'Colours of the day' that Coastal Command planes had been taught to fire upwards as they first approached an Allied convoy or Escort Group. Plane captains, also, had learnt their lesson. No experienced pilot came too close to an Allied ship even after having fired off the correct colours of the day. Quite a few Coastal Command planes had been shot at, and one or two shot down, by the worried gunners below and tales had drifted back to the Command's Messes. In any case there was no need actually to overfly any vessel.

No 6 received the accustomed full quota of 20mm shells and once again the reporting procedures were commenced. But not for long. Fifty-five minutes later, No 7 was sighted. Once again it was the usual contest to see whether cannons could be fired before the U-boat could retreat under the waves. Once more 15 rounds from each gun spattered into the sea around the disappearing U-boat. Once more the wireless crackled with its reports. Once more the SNO was approached and informed and probably once more the SNO almost kicked himself with frustration; angry that he hadn't a dozen more ships under his command so that he could send one each time to where the the enemy had dived. Given unlimited time to 'out-sit' the U-boat, an escort vessel could, as likely as not, win the inevitable cat-and-mouse game that a smart U-boat commander would play with the enemy overhead. Never enough ships: never enough time! With a bare six escorts at his disposal, all were needed to guard the convoy's flanks. *More* than six were really needed even for this, bearing in mind that 30-40 ships required protection.

Back in Iceland as the reports of the attacks were received, some even began to wonder if some kind of bizarre trick was being played. Terry Bulloch had a reputation for being unorthodox. Was this his way of checking up to see how alert they were at base?

It was by then approaching dusk. The sun does not stay out overlong in the Northern latitudes approaching the shortest day of the year. This was the time when U-boats normally began to close the convoy for attack at night. Wizz Isted would have been airborne for some hours as the time for Terry to depart approached.

Before half an hour had passed, No 8 was sighted. The flight-engineer had, luckily, found another clip of ammunition. Once more the big Lib was sent hurtling seawards. This U-boat was slow to respond and as the plane passed over it, the tail gunner was able to blast it with 100 rounds of ·303 ammunition from his machine guns. This would have hardly marked the tough steel hull but it made him feel good. Up to that point he had not been able to contribute to any of the previous attacks. It agonised the Bull that he had no depth-charge to drop. This time he had achieved almost total surprise and the U-boat was on the surface just asking to be sunk.

Back at base he lamented: 'It was a sitter. If I'd had any depth-charges left, it would have been a dead duck.' Some would have been satisfied with what he had already accomplished but not the Bull. He had good reason to hate the Hun and would have gladly slaughtered the lot.

As had been planned, Wizz Isted duly arrived to take over from Terry. By the time that he departed from Iceland, the convoy had moved closer to that island and, with less mileage to cover, Wizz had managed to get ten depth-charges within the plane's bomb bay. He had received most of the reports of the attacks that his flight commander was making and was determined to be as prepared as possible for similar successes. Nor was he to be disappointed. Before he, too, was reluctantly obliged to turn back for the homeward flight, he had tracked down a further five U-boats and had attacked two. On the first he dropped nine of his 'dustbins' of explosives and dropped his remaining one on his third sighting. As usual the results were inconclusive; especially in the dark. By all normal standards, Wizz's feat of forcing five U-boats to dive in the course of a single sortie, would have gone into the record book and remained for all time but, coming as they did immediately after Terry's eight attacks, they lost out by comparison.

Between them Terry and Wizz had forced no less than 13 U-boats to dive and to lose contact with the convoy. They had broken up what otherwise would in all probability have been the most damaging attack of the war. Never before had Doenitz managed to get 22 U-boats into attacking positions against a single convoy. And he had passed up the opportunity to attack the slow SC111 to do so. Perhaps most damaging of all was the effect of these attacks on the morale of his U-boat crews. Most were new to the game. His three great aces, Commanders Kretschmer, Prien and Schepke, each a German hero known to every boy in the Fatherland, were by 1942 all gone. The latter two killed and the former captured. Their replacements were equally determined and bold but lacked the experience. Being attacked in what was, they had been assured, a 'safe' area took an edge from their keenness. Instead of 8 and 9 December being historic days to be remembered by every U-boat crewman, and also by the nation at large, it marked the day when the U-boats began to lose the war for Europe. November 1942 proved to be a turning point in the U-boat war. Six grim savage months lay ahead before Doenitz withdrew from the Atlantic routes, but never again did sinkings by U-boats reach the tonnage of that terrible month. And never after 8 December could the U-boat commanders feel safe in the Gap. Thereafter, although they did

The Day to Remember. The corvette *Potentilla* reaches the scene of the destruction of *U-254*.

Two depth charges enter the water on the next attack at position 57°37′N 34°33′W.

The depth charge explosions along the track of the U-boat, on the same attack.

Attack at position 57°37′N 34°33′W continued.

The explosions subsiding and the U-boat track.

their best to emulate the great Kretschmer* and Co, they had, metaphorically, forever to look over their shoulders. Their numbers steadily increased. More and more anti-aircraft guns were added to their crafts. New scientific devices were added to help them detect their enemy from above, but over all their sinkings steadily decreased, (although there was an alarm in March 1943 when losses rose dramatically).

By the time that the Bull landed his Liberator safely back in Iceland on that memorable day, successfully combating the usual foul weather, he and his crew had been in the air for nearly 17 hours, including about eight spent around HX217. In all they had been on duty the best part of 24 hours.

The real proof of their accomplishments came that night in the Gap. Conditions were right for the U-boats to attack. However the attackers had been thrown into disarray. Their very positions had been revealed. The naval escorts had been heartened by the success of the two planes and were determined to show that they too could fight off U-boats. In numbers, they were woefully few: just a destroyer, HMS *Flame*, the Polish destroyer *Burza* and four slow corvettes, the *Potentilla*, the *Eglantine* and the *Rose*, all three Norwegian, and HMS *Vervian*. Between them they made many other U-boat sightings. What they lacked in quantity, they made up by quality. They had their tails up, much as the underwater enemy had theirs down. A number of attacks were made that night upon the convoy but not with the usual Germanic determination. Each attack was beaten off. The U-boats had had enough. Many had lost the scent and some showed no great inclination to regain it. One ship was lost in the early hours of 9 December but that was all.

By 10 December, the convoy was within range of the many Hudsons, Flying Fortresses and other Coastal Command planes based in the UK. Some American Catalina flying boats from Sullom

---

* Otto Kretschmer was Germany's top scoring U-boat ace of the war. In some respects he was Terry Bulloch's opposite number in the Battle of the Atlantic. He was a perfectionist who used coolness, imagination and daring to devise new methods of attacking Allied ships. Like Terry Bulloch also, he achieved his successes relatively early in the war. He showed the way and was an inspiration and byword for those who came later. Although taken prisoner in 1941 when *U-99* was depth-charged to the surface by the Royal Navy, his total of tonnage sunk was never surpassed. Still alive, and a retired admiral, he has corresponded in friendly terms with the author.

Voe also joined in the hunt. As a result, for the next three days, U-boats continued to be located and attacked from the air. One of these planes even saw two but never again did one crew detect eight on a single sortie or even five, as Squadron Leader Isted had done.

Nor was it just HX217 that was saved. The slower and more vulnerable SC111, crossing on the more direct Great Circle track (HX217 sailed about 100 miles north of this), escaped without a single casualty. In all it was almost three weeks at sea in an area infested by U-boats. The total score to Doenitz was just two out of about 90 ships, counting escorts. His losses were: for sure *U-254*, attacked by Terry, and up to half a dozen others claimed as probables or damaged. As usual, it was impossible to tell. Most U-boats soon turned for home. There was damage to repair; also they had expended a lot of precious fuel in their dash from their normal stations to reach in time assigned positions in the Gap where the wolf packs were supposed to tear the enemy to bits. As one commentator put it: 'The size of the food ration in Britain that winter depended upon the arrival of those convoys.' They and Britain survived.

The Bull had been awarded a Distinguished Service Order only five days before setting out to protect HX217. To the surprise of none, he was awarded a Bar to his DSO for this outstanding work. Michael Layton was also awarded a DSO, one of the very few navigators to earn this exceptional award. Such was his known skill that, earlier, he had been detailed to navigate the Liberator in which Churchill had first flown to Moscow.

It was a quite remarkable achievement for the Bull to have been awarded two DSOs within a week or so of each other. The C-in-C of Coastal Command ACM Sir Philip Joubert de la Ferté summed it up in his signal of 9 December to AOC Iceland:

Please convey my warmest congratulations to the Captain and aircrew of B120 for their magnificent day's work on December 8 in support of Convoy HX217. They showed the greatest skill and determination in making depth-charge and cannon attacks ... and their efforts were crowned by the destruction of a U-boat which was confirmed by surface craft ... while all share the success, I wish you to convey my special congratulations to S/Ldr Bulloch and his navigator F/O Layton.

Similar signals were sent to Bulloch and his crew by AOC Iceland, the Commanding Officer of 120 Squadron back at Nutts Corner and most generously by the Admiralty which freely acknowledged the part played by this crew of Coastal Command. All stressed that the efforts of Terry and his crew (backed up by those of Isted and his crew) had saved the convoy.

For a month, the news was kept to official circles. This was a calculated policy. Whenever a U-boat was lost, and in this case the losses were probably more than one, it would be left to Doenitz to find out the slow painful way. As his signals went from U-boat Command to his boats at sea and were unanswered, bit by bit the truth would be sinking in. It hurt the Admiral, too. He personally knew virtually all his U-boat commanders. It was best therefore to hold back news of positive killings and to let him hope, and suffer, in vain. The destruction of *his* morale was of vital importance. Only he could make such momentous decisions as that which he eventually made: to withdraw U-boats from North Atlantic operations and thus leave open Britain's lifeline to the New World and all its riches.

The award to Squadron Leader Bulloch of the Bar to his DSO was not announced until 10 January and when it was publicised it came with an unusual amount of detail. By then Terry was familiar with the formal preamble. It was the fourth time he had had reason to enjoy the words: 'His Majesty King George VI, on the recommendation of the Air Officer Commanding Coastal Command has graciously been pleased ...' What was unexpected, however, was the newspaper publicity that attended the award announcement. It was mid-winter 1942/3 and the war was at a watershed. The glory of the Battle of Britain had faded into memory but the German reverses in Russia in late 1941 and in late 1942 were signs that the war might turn in the Allies' favour. The much hoped for 'Second Front', i.e. the reconquest of Europe across the Channel was still 18 months into the future, but the British victory at Alamein, in the Western Desert, was a much needed boost. With it came Operation Torch, the Anglo American landings in North Africa. The nation was in a mood for heroes and the press had been given a new one in Terry. They made the most of it. Because of its secret equipment Coastal Command rarely gave the press any news.

It preferred to work quietly and to keep their enemy guessing. This time, however, they revealed practically all.

Every paper in the land welcomed the unexpected bonanza with open arms. 'The Bull gets a U-boat' was one headline. A more sober one was 'Ulsterman's success, RAF Terrors decorated.' This reflected the point that Isted had also been decorated. Wizz received a well earned Distinguished Flying Cross (DFC). Another read, 'Atlantic convoy gets through' and another 'Belfast ace sinks two U-boats' (Trust the Press to overdo it!). 'Epic defence by escorts' rightly emphasised that this was a joint RAF/RN victory. 'A lesson for the subs': this from a Montreal paper; the town from which Layton came. 'Belfast ace sinks two, hits five'. 'Sub smashers win 5 awards in big convoy fight'. This last reflected the point that, in addition to Isted and Layton, both Ginger Turner and Jock McColl had been awarded the DFM (Distinguished Flying Medal). Another headline was 'Atlantic convoy fights off 35 U-boat attacks.' They had arrived at this number by including every sighting since the ships had left Halifax on 1 December. 'U-boat Packs Routed in Atlantic Battle' was accurate. 'One bomber hits seven subs' was perhaps less so. 'Dinner plates went up. U-boats went down. British ace-hunter's thrilling story' etc. Even the glossy weekly papers got into the act. Excellent pictures were reproduced of an actual U-boat attack in both the *Sphere* and the *Illustrated London News*. The pictures had been taken by McColl during a previous U-boat attack. Nor was this all. The Bull was long overdue an operational rest, so the Command grounded him and used him to tell his own tale over the radio. His BBC account was typical of the man: terse, modest and much to the point. He said:

'Almost at once we struck lucky. Astern of the ships and on the Liberator's port beam I spotted a sub travelling just on the surface. It was going all out to catch up with the convoy. I got into position to attack and just as we dived on it, the submarine began to go down in a hurry. I didn't see what happened after the depth charges were dropped. My navigator told me they straddled the sub and hid it in showers of spray.'

Michael Layton was also put on the air to finish the description as he had been in the astrodome and had had an excellent view. The Bull also related that the corvette *Potentilla* had flashed him three messages: 'You certainly got him': 'Parts of dead bodies seen' and 'You killed him'.

December 8 1942 was a memorable day. Its like would never be repeated. As the official Coastal Command report reads: 'A study of HX217 and SC111 shows air and sea cover at its best. In consequence, U-boats were destroyed and the convoys brought safely to port in the face of the most determined opposition yet encountered.'

A further 615 U-boats would be commissioned and built before the war finally drew to a close and Doenitz never wavered from the belief, well founded, that he had stated in January 1942:

'Whatever the course of, and end of, the Russian campaign may be, the war against the Anglo-Saxon power will be decided at sea … it is only with the U-boat arm that we can take the offensive.' Some on our side thought the same. One of our war leaders expressed almost the same when he wrote: 'It is on the sea and only on the sea that we can lose this war.'

History has confirmed both statements. Doenitz's U-boat arm might have proved to be decisive but, as the war progressed, that arm was being progressively twisted. One of the principal twisters was Squadron Leader Terence Malcolm Bulloch, DSO and Bar, DFC and Bar – the Bull with the Hawkseyes, the Ulsterman to whom flying was life: to whom revenge was sweet and to whom the war meant 'kill or be killed' and whose only desire was to be in the thick of it: leading from the front.

CHAPTER TWO

Early Days

The Belfast where Terence Malcolm Bulloch spent his childhood was a more peaceful place than the Belfast of the 1970s and 1980s. And in Belfast, few places were more peaceful than Malone Park, the tree-lined avenue where the Bulloch family lived. Young Malcolm, as he was called at home, was aged three or four when the family moved to Belfast from Lisburn, a busy market town a dozen miles to the south. The family consisted of the parents, a brother three years older and Malcolm's twin sister Yvonne. The twins were born on 16 February 1916. The brother had the unusual names of Hugh Larmor McLearn and was known as Larmor. The father, Samuel Bulloch, was a man of varied interests. For a living he was 'something in the linen trade': something fairly profitable, too. Synthetic fabrics were largely unknown and the linen industry was profitable and stable throughout Northern Ireland. The Bullochs were comfortably well-off without any pretensions of great wealth. In many respects they were typical of the middle-class, non-religious Protestant families which constituted the backbone of Ulster. While being Protestants, they held no fanatical beliefs or sectarian views.

Outside his work, Samuel Bulloch had leanings towards the dramatic arts. For many years he produced radio plays for the BBC Northern Ireland service. Generally, he seems to have given a lot of his time to outside interests. Such people, if efficient and amiable, are apt to be appointed 'Hon Sec' or 'Hon Treasurer' of various non-profit organisations. He appears to have held such positions for the local Shakespearian Society, the Irish Hockey Union – a game at which he had represented his country, and the local Reform Club. A person who knew the family well has volunteered that: 'Malcolm's father was not too visible at home. He appeared to be quite 'arty' and was away a lot on mysterious acting missions etc.'

A largely absent father was reasonably commonplace in those

days. It was an era when middle-class children were largely brought up by a succession of nannies with the parents only entering their lives in fits and starts. Mothers naturally played a major role but fathers tended to be distant figures of kindly authority, especially during the children's early years. Later their influence became more significant.

The Bullochs had originally come from Scotland. However they had lived in Ulster for so many generations that they regarded themselves as Loyalist Irishmen. Samuel Bulloch was staunchly British. He was one of those Ulstermen who, just prior to the First World War at a time when the Parliament in Westminster were planning to give Ireland home rule which would have meant Ulster coming under a Dublin government, had joined the Ulster Volunteers. 'You abandon us to the South at your peril' was their cry. So they armed themselves (with German rifles) and were prepared to fight the Englishmen who were proposing to make them less British. Irish politics were never simple.

Elsie Bulloch, Terry's mother, was descended from sturdy Huguenot stock. Her family had also been in Ireland for many generations. Her ancestors had fled their native France when the great Edict of Nantes had been rescinded. After this French Protestants could no longer feel secure from religious percecution. Elsie Bulloch was known and respected locally as a forceful character. One who knew her has described her in picturesque terms: 'She strode about Malone Park with a purposeful air ... She was a down-to-earth woman who walked as if it was going out of fashion and golfed in the same vigorous way.' Like her younger son, she was a very determined person. 'Although she could easily afford a caddy (then 6d or 9d per round), she carried her own clubs.'

Golf became a favourite game for all the Bullochs. Samuel Bulloch showed much the same form at this as he had, earlier, on the hockey pitch. The children all played. It was probably one of the few times that they spent long periods with their father. In the home, Elsie Bulloch was not a person to be trifled with, as young Malcolm soon found out. However her strong will was matched by that of her younger son. As Malcolm's twin sister recalls: 'Malcolm took after mummy.' From an early age, he knew what it was that he wanted and what he considered to be right. Once he had made up his mind, that was the end of the matter. 'No matter how often she punished him, it made not the slightest difference.'

The Bulloch family, despite these occasional clashes of wills, was by all accounts a happy and stable one. The three children got on well together under the kindly leadership of Larmor. As Yvonne remembers it: 'The two boys were so different in character that they seldom clashed.' Neither envy nor jealousy separated them. Larmor had inherited the social affability of his father whereas Malcolm, while possessing many of his mother's sterling qualities, was handicapped socially by being almost excessively shy. For this reason he firmly refused to take part in those activities which involved mixing with strangers. He refused to learn to play whist or bridge and nothing could persuade him to join in dancing classes or to go to children's parties. Girls were definitely not to his tastes.

Elsie Bulloch, for all her strong-minded views and her clashes with her younger son, was a kindly and responsible mother. In her eyes Malcolm seemed delicate and needed building up. She fed him extra milk and eggs. She also assiduously rubbed his chest with camphorated oil. It is easy to imagine that the young lad, who from an early age spent much of his time reading adventure and historical stories, was highly resentful of the imputation that he needed to be built up. His instincts were already telling him that he was tougher than most. Yet his sister recalls: 'Mummy thought him too thin. She said his ribs were like washboards.' Like the son who took after her, she probably set her sights at the highest marks.

Their nannies operated on sound but simple principles. Nannies in those days saw to it that their charges were brought up to adhere to the virtues of cleanliness, honesty and fair play with the vague figure of an awesome God never far away: a God who saw all. Next to him stood King George.

The children were not sent to Sunday school, nor were they obliged to go to church on Sundays, except for special services at Christmas and Easter. In this respect, they followed the pattern of most English Protestants. As was the custom of the times, their nannies saw to it that the children said their prayers on their knees alongside their beds each night. 'God bless mummy and daddy, sister and brother' and 'Thank you God for another day'. It was essential to keep in favour with God. He was well aware of your transgressions but, being fair, also noted your good deeds of the day.

Households such as the Bullochs' always had two or more maids. They were nearly always Catholics; probably the only ones that the children ever met. This was not a sign of a ruling Protestant majority lording it over a slave minority. It came about because the Catholic families tended to have larger families: often too large for their homes. Maids invariably lived in the houses of their employers and this eased the congestion at their homes. Maids were kindly treated, paid a small sum, were given the opportunity to see how other, more wealthy, ran their homes and, most important of all, found opportunities to meet boys from a different area. Consequently many left to get married and to start families of their own from the lessons they had learned. The children generally got on well with the maids and vice versa.

At an early age the twins were sent to a small private kindergarten within walking distance of Malone Park. When it was wet, they were given a penny for the tram ride. Malcolm alone would save his penny and would walk in defiance of the weather. It was as if he was determined to show the world that he was *not* delicate. At this private school, the twins met and became friends with a boy of similar age. Howard Smith was born on 13 February 1916 three days before the twins. Howard and Malcolm were to remain friends for many years. At the kindergarten, the children learnt the three Rs along with some singing and good manners. The firm but kindly discipline of the times was further enforced.

Malone Park was a charming place. It was a private avenue not open to through traffic. Red brick pillars guarded one entrance and to ensure its status of a private road, this entrance could be sealed off by gates which, to abide by the law, would be closed on one day each year. The residents were responsible for the upkeep of the road.

In the 1920s, Malone Park, on the perimeter of Belfast, was within sight of parks and green fields. There was a cinder track which connected it with Upper Malone Road and the children used to ride their bikes along it with freedom as it was not suitable for heavier traffic. Across the road, where new housing estates now exist, were open fields. The boys with their air guns could here take pot shots at rabbits and rats in the ditches. Naturally such a household had a much loved dog.

At the age of only seven, Malcolm was packed off to a preparatory boarding school. This was Mourne Grange. It was some distance from Belfast and stood in splendid grounds at the foot of the famous Mountains of Mourne that 'sweep down to the sea'. Howard Smith was dispatched there at the same time. He has confessed to feeling very homesick and comments that Malcolm seemed less affected.

Mourne Grange prided itself upon its high standards of scholarship, games, gym and school plays. This last may have been why the father had selected it for his boys. From an early age, Larmor had showed signs of sharing his father's delight of acting and as he had been sent there, it was natural for the younger brother to follow in Larmor's footsteps. All the pupils came from Protestant homes and several came from the South. For the first time in his life Malcolm had regularly to attend church on Sundays. The school must have acquired quite a reputation as some boys came from homes 'over the water' in England. It had been founded by Allan Carey and had rapidly expanded. It prepared boys for the better known Public Schools in England and for the few in Northern Ireland of comparable standing.

Young Malcolm's shyness probably helped to keep him clear of trouble. He appears to have settled down quickly. At Mourne Grange his aptitude and keenness for games soon showed. Apart from making him popular, this emphasises a strong trait which has remained with Terry Bulloch to this day, namely his intense loyalty to whatever team or side he belonged.

Young Malcolm threw himself into all the school games with tremendous energy. Possibly he was trying to prove to all that he was far from being delicate: a word he greatly disliked. At school work, he found it hard to keep up with the very high standards that Mourne Grange required. Fortunately, hard work has never bothered Terence Malcolm Bulloch. It is a challenge to which he responds.

While at Mourne Grange he became for a while an ardent cricket fan and, during the holidays, kept the scores of all the English county games as reported in the daily papers. Ireland has few cricket heroes of its own, so Hobbs and Sutcliffe, Woolley and Hendren, Tate and Rhodes joined the list of great historical names that crowded young Malcolm's mind. He also played the game with his usual determination. By dint of persevering he became a useful bowler and in his last year took 32 wickets in school matches. The school magazine also describes him as: 'A forcing bat though lacking style.' That fits. There was never any doubt in later life about TMB being forceful. His entry into Mourne Grange adds that: 'He is to be given pocket money of between 3d and 6d per week according to his work and conduct.' Mourne Grange with its 'Stick and Carrot' methods of extracting the best from its pupils, seems to have done Malcolm nothing but good although his father may have been a mite disappointed that only his elder son paid full attention to opportunities that the school gave to those interested in acting. Larmor probably learnt some basic stage techniques there. Later in life he would take part in some of the plays which father produced for the BBC.

Malcolm, like his mother, kept both feet planted solidly on the ground. Play acting was not for him. As Howard Smith does not comment upon Malcolm's shyness at school, it would appear that it was beginning to evaporate. Possibly the fact that he was part of an all male environment might be a reason? His shyness might have been principally evident in the presence of girls? From an early age, TMB appears to have been 'a man's man' and proud of it.

The departure of Malcolm, to a boarding school broke the close ties which had existed between the twins. Possibly his mother planned it this way? She strode about like a man and must have been delighted that she had borne such a determined masculine son. After Mourne Grange had separated them, Yvonne only played with her brothers during the school holidays. Although they were at the same school, Mourne Grange also separated Malcolm from Larmor. New boys were rapidly taught their place and Bulloch II learnt that he and Bulloch I were poles apart in the school's pecking order. Surnames only were used and it is doubtful if anyone, other than Howard Smith, knew the Christian names of either Bulloch.

For the long summer holidays, the family would spend a week or more at the seaside at Castlerock. Here, Larmor and Yvonne made the most of the chance to bathe and frolic in the sea but Malcolm obstinately refused to learn to swim. Possibly he felt shy at having to undress, more or less in the open, on the beach. His shyness with strangers also tended to keep him apart from other children also enjoying their annual visit to the seaside. Yet it is possible that these visits could have been the initial inspiration for his life-long love affair with flying. Any boy with his exceptional eyesight could hardly fail to be fascinated by the sea birds which are evident in such numbers off that coast. As well as the ever-present graceful gulls, there were the more spectacular diving cormorants and gannets. There were also the wheeling terns and the big gliding pelicans silently riding the rising upcurrents. While the other two would be in the sea, building sand castles or making new acquaintances, Malcolm might be found reading a book which was sure to be an adventure book or one about some famous British hero. One who knew him well during this period has described him as: 'A bit of a loner.'

Historical figures have always interested TMB: both real and fictional. Nelson and Drake were admired along with Robin Hood and King Arthur and his gallant knights. Young Malcolm also collected stamps with more than a youngster's usual interest. Here his inherent neatness came into play. His albums were as meticulously kept as, in later life, were his RAF log books.

Physically he appears to have benefited from his mother's early concern. No longer were his ribs like washboards. From Prep School days onwards, TMB has kept himself in good physical shape. As his sister affirms, 'Malcolm was always in training for some sporting event and he never smoked cigarettes.' Although the lung cancer scare had not even reared its head above the horizon, there was the belief that cigarettes were bad for some, especially sportsmen – 'Bad for the wind' – so those who wished to excel at games, kept clear of them.

It is difficult to imagine that Malcolm did not envy the easy social graces of his elder brother, but Yvonne is positive on this point. None could resent Larmor. He enjoyed everything he did whether he did it well or not. Moreover he was prepared to try his hand at anything. Malcolm, by contrast, was selective. He only exerted himself at those pastimes which seemed best to suit him and when he took up a hobby or sport it was with the determination to excel.

He refused to learn to ice-skate or to learn to ride a horse and he would have nothing whatever to do with dancing classes. Too 'cissy' perhaps? However he took to golf and worked at it. With him it had to be all or nothing. He was never one to dabble.

Both boys had to apply themselves diligently to keep up to the high standards of school work that Mourne Grange demanded. Of the two, Yvonne believes that Malcolm was naturally the brighter: also, in her eyes, the better-looking. By dint of hard work and some extra coaching in maths, both brothers duly passed the Common Entrance examinations. This opened the door to the better public schools. Mourne Grange sent boys to many of the best schools in England but Samuel Bulloch, perhaps mindful of the 'perfidy' of England which had driven him take up arms against her, selected Campbell College, in Belfast, for both his sons. This was as good as any English school and probably the best in all Ireland. It stood in splendid grounds on the Eastern edge of the town, adjacent to Stormont Castle, the seat of Government in Northern Ireland.

Campbell College, like all public schools of the time, was largely controlled and disciplined by the prefects – the senior boys (up to aged 19) who had achieved distinctions at work and/or games. These 'Lords of the School' had private studies and at Campbell College, were simply known as 'the Studies'. The masters often chose to turn a blind eye to the harsh disciplinary measures that the Studies used to keep the juniors in order. The boys soon learnt to tread carefully in the presence of the Studies.

Malcolm again rapidly settled down at Campbell College. No doubt the considerate Larmor, who was already at the school warned him what to expect. Larmor had made a name for himself at the school by his skill as a marksman. Not only was he the crack-shot of the shooting team but he had scored so well in inter-school matches that he had been chosen to shoot in Canada as part of an 'English Schools' team: no mean feat for an Irish boy at an Ulster school. Moreover, in Canada, he had proved to be the star of the competition and might have been described as the junior crack-shot of the British Empire. Otherwise Larmor took part in games in rather cavalier fashion. He took them as they came and enjoyed them without any great attempt to excel.

Once again Malcolm became Bulloch II and his path at school

seldom crossed that of Bulloch I. Public Schools had a strict hierarchical structure which went into many aspects designed to keep the 'new bugs' in their place. Juniors were not even allowed to dress in style and had to keep their hands well clear of their pockets. As they advanced up the ladder certain additional dress laxities were permitted. If they reached the Studies, they could really swagger around. Again the stick-and-carrot approach.

Campbell was British, but not necessarily English, to the core. As with all public schools, it was where many Service officers had their first taste of military training. It maintained a nominally voluntary Officers Training Corps (OTC) into which enrolment was virtually compulsory. This became for many the stepping stone to a subsequent career in the British Army. Tradition had not really caught up and neither the Navy nor the relatively new Royal Air Force came into the Service training offered by the OTC. The corps was highly regarded and Malcolm threw himself into its drills, parades and long marches with enthusiasm. For one thing, it was a means of demonstrating how tough and endurable he had become. For another, anything taken so seriously was an attraction to him.

All the Bulloch family were musical to some degree or other. It was a characteristic passed down by Mrs Bulloch. Malcolm, with his eyes on the prestigious OTC, took up the Irish Pipes. With his customary determination to 'do the thing properly', he soon gained a place in the school band which figured prominently at all OTC parades. Before he was to leave, he had become its leader with the title of Pipe Major. The Irish pipes mean almost as much to an Ulsterman as do the Scottish ones to a Scot and it can be imagined that father Bulloch was rightly proud of his Pipe Major son.

Larmor had set his sights on becoming an Army officer. His great skill as a marksman placed him in an advantageous position. Malcolm, seldom one to take the same line as his elder brother, was too fascinated by flying to consider this as a career. This fascination of his took a positive shape when, at Campbell College, a lecture was given by a visiting squadron leader from Ulster's own Auxiliary Squadron.

After the lecture, a few selected boys were given a flight in an ancient RAF biplane. Although it was, as Terry Bulloch now recalls, a bit draughty and very noisy, it nevertheless left an indelible impression. Up to that point, while the young Malcolm had been 'mad' about flying and had remained so for several years, the definite decision to put all his considerable energies towards a career in the RAF stems from that visit and flight. Flying also had a well publicised civil side and young Bulloch was familiar with the names of the civil aces of those days: the Mollisons (Amy Johnson and her husband): Sir Alan Cobham, Kingsford-Smith, Lindbergh etc. Who knows, if instead a famous civilian pilot had visited the school, Malcolm, at the impressionable age that he was, might have bent his energies in that direction?

Always one to take a matter seriously, a fellow student recalls TMB asking questions of another visiting lecturer about whether the League of Nations had considered forming its own air force with which to help to keep the peace in a world which was already showing signs of plunging itself into another global conflict. This is interesting because it shows that the teenager was concerning himself with major political issues likely to upset the status quo of the country he had come to admire and respect. Never one to extol the English as such, TMB has a strong feeling for the British way of life and, as he showed in the years to come, was prepared to risk his life to defend that way of living.

Games figured prominently in Malcolm's schooldays at Campbell College. With his love of physical fitness, he took to Rugger like a duck to water. Although never above average height or weight, he made up for his lack of inches by fearless courage and fanatical determination. One who shared those days with him has described his performance on the rugger field as 'maniacal'. He also took up boxing and earned school colours at this. The once delicate lad whom his mother had built up so lovingly, seemed determined never again to be regarded as anything less than indestructible. He had changed. Even his name was changing. 'Malcolm' was fast disappearing. Christian names were not used at school but TMB let it be known where they were used that henceforth he would be 'Terry': and so it has been ever since.'*

* A few in the RAF knew him as 'Tim': an obvious running together of his two initials 'T' and 'M'.

Terry Bulloch has always been touchy about his names. A common error is to spell it Bullo*ck*. This still rouses him to instant fury. One of his former schoolmates recalls that in a school boxing match, he was incorrectly announced as 'T.M. Bewlosh of Campbell College'. This must have roused his ire, as the account of the fight in the school magazine reads: 'Good (Malone Training School) v Bulloch (Campbell College). The fight proceeded briskly with Good getting the better of it but after about 15 seconds, Bulloch landed a short right to the jaw and that was the end of it.'

At rugger he was in the first XV for two years. It is typical of the brothers that Larmor was quite happy to have been in the third XV although obviously having at least equal talent judged by the fact that later he represented Northern Ireland.

For all his toughness, there was another side to the ultra tough Bulloch II. While Pipe Major, he was extremely helpful to the juniors learning the ropes. Another characteristic was that he was extremely punctual and never the slightest bit sloppy in appearance. He would be up early, well before the time for breakfast at school. With a book in hand (still an avid reader), he would stand on the landing and shout a warning to the latecomers:

> He would be standing at the junction where the back corridors form a T. He would be alone, always reading a book. When a master appeared and signalled the boys in to breakfast, Bulloch's shout of 'Going in' would alert those not so spry as he was at getting up in the morning. Boys would come tumbling down the stairs making last minute adjustments to ties, collars and jackets and sometimes shoving socks in their pockets to be put on later. The number of boys who were prevented from being late thanks to Bulloch's timely shout must, over the years, be reckoned in scores.

The same fellow student also remembers Bulloch II's rare appearance in a school play. He was cast in the part of the villain in *The Man in the Bowler Hat*, which he describes as one of the worst plays ever written. The performance was a disaster. The leading character, the Man in the Bowler Hat, muffed his lines and as these

Out for a picnic at half term from Mourne Grange prep school. Larmor is standing on the mudguard, the twins, Terry and Yvonne, and Howard sitting.

Pipe Major Bulloch at the planting of a tree on Empire Day, 1935.

Campbell College, Belfast.

The Rugger XV at Campbell College. Terry is far left, middle row.

formed the dénouement of the play, this torpedoed the whole thing. This appears to have been TMB's only attempt to emulate his father's thespian inclinations. However his habit of reading led to him being appointed library curator in his final year at school. He also became one of the editors of the school magazine, *The Campbellian*.

As well as always being neatly dressed, an unusual characteristic for one who took so much pride in being the toughest of the tough was that his nails were always kept in good trim. It being added by this observer, 'Not that there was anything the slightest bit soft about him: quite the contrary, in fact.' The picture of a perfectionist emerges. If a job had to be done, then it had to be done properly. It was a concept that he certainly maintained throughout the war.

One of the duties of the Pipe Major was to lead the band on parades. Here he had the onerous task of tossing the mace skywards and catching it on its return. The Reverend David Erskine, then a junior whom Terry helped a lot when first joining the band, recalls that he never once dropped it on ceremonial occasions. He also mentions that the boy who took over from Terry dropped it all over the place and quite seriously damaged it. Terry was to show later that he had exceptional eyesight and this may have helped. It also shows that he was a man for the big occasions and that he took his responsibilities seriously.

As had been the case at Mourne Grange, Campbell College seems to have developed Terry Bulloch along all the right lines. The firm discipline helped to bring the best from a person of his dedication and it was helpful to him that, long before he was due to leave, he had made up his mind what he wanted to do with the rest of his life. Purposefulness helps a lot when undergoing a standard routine. He knew how to pick and choose those subjects that would serve him best in the RAF later in life. As Yvonne has remarked: 'Malcolm can rarely be shaken from his own ideas.' It was his idea to fly planes for the RAF.

Although the maths again proved arduous, TMB duly passed the stiff entrance examination to Cranwell College, the RAF Officer's training college. All he now had to do was to pass the severe medical examination but, in his mind, he knew that few if any at school were as fit as he. But Fate was to play him a trick: a cruel blow that would have shattered a man with lesser determination: one which would have made others give up all thoughts of ever becoming a pilot and an officer in such a demanding service as the RAF.

CHAPTER THREE

A Set-back

The step which Terry Bulloch, aged 18, had to take in order to qualify for Cranwell College seemed simple enough. All he had to do was to pass the RAF pilot's medical examination. For one as fit as he was, it seemed a 'piece of cake'. He didn't smoke; he was not a heavy drinker. His toughness and durability were well known at Campbell College. To his surprise and great disappointment, the Medical Board turned him down and all because he happened to have a swollen gland in his neck. In other important aspects he passed with flying colours. To have been failed because of what seemed to him to be a technicality made the rejection more difficult to bear.

Ever since that visiting squadron leader had lectured at Campbell College, Terry had had but one objective; to join the RAF as a pilot. He had never tried harder and had become used to achieving whatever he set out to accomplish. The blow was almost shattering. He felt confident that he possessed the required qualities of courage, eyesight and judgement. For years he had read everything he could about the planes flown by the RAF. He was familiar with the names of some who flew them, such as the pilots of the high-speed flight who had won the Schneider Trophy for Britain and then gone on to capture the world speed record. The Supermarine float planes they used had raised this to just over 400 mph: then the fastest speed ever reached by man.

It was a disappointment to his father, too. He had noted his son's interest in aviation and had arranged, via a friend in London, to have the aviation magazines sent to the house in Malone Park. Some instinct told Terry Bulloch that the RAF was for him and he for them. The air was a place where Britain still ruled supreme and the RAF was one shining example of it. He wanted to be part of that success.

Terry was not to be thwarted by such a trivial thing as a swollen gland. It would have to be treated or removed. The family doctor came and in due course the trouble was traced and the swelling disappeared. But all this took time. Moreover the doctor could not guarantee that the trouble might not recur. A further delay was that the RAF Medical Board would not retest Terry for many months just in case the trouble did again appear.

This was a frustrating time for the young man. His fellow schoolmates had gone on to their respective courses: to the universities, to Sandhurst etc. He alone was left cooling his heels impatiently. Patience was never a virtue of the younger Bulloch son. Larmor, as usual, was kind and sympathetic. He had acquired a small Austin 7 and in this he taught both Terry and Yvonne to drive. It was before the days when driving tests were compulsory. One simply applied for a licence, paid five shillings and drove as best one could.

In due course, the Medical Board agreed to retest Terry. He passed without difficulty. However a new difficulty arose: a more serious one, too. Owing to the lapse of time between the two medical examinations, Terry now found himself too old to be admitted to Cranwell. Nor could the Powers that-be be persuaded to make an exception. Many wanted to join the RAF and, with Government cuts on defence being imposed by Parliament the numbers had to be kept to a minimum. This left Terry out on a limb. He could, perhaps, have been accepted by a university. He might perhaps have been found a job in his father's linen trade. He wanted none of these things. He wanted to fly.

Near Belfast there was a small grass airfield which did, or had, belonged to Lord Londonderry. It was at Newtownards. It was used by a few small civil planes. Terry managed to find himself a job of sorts there. It was neither exciting nor exacting employment. He became a sort of odd-job boy: timekeeping and the like. At least it took him near to planes.

At Newtownards his enthusiasm and knowledge of aviation matters won him the respect of some of the pilots who flew from its rough grass field. When able to do so, some began to take him with them on their local flights and, finding out that he knew all about the theory of flight, they, unofficially, allowed him to handle the controls. As Yvonne has said: 'I'm sure that he knew how to fly a plane and could have done so. He had read so much about it.' However on the whole this must have been one of the blackest and most frustrating periods of Terry's life. He was not the sort to relish failure.

Fate, however, was to give the young man a second chance to become an RAF pilot. Indirectly, he would have to thank the aggressive dictators of Europe. The strutting Mussolini in Italy and the even more bellicose Hitler were assuming such threatening postures that even Britain, which had been slumbering for years in the belief that these unbalanced men would ultimately calm down and become 'gentlemen', felt the need to re-arm: and to do so with urgency to make up for the years of earlier neglect. Winston Churchill, then totally out of office and favour, had persistently drawn attention to the need to create an airforce comparable to the Italian and German ones.

Thanks to Churchill and others the decision was made to increase the size of the RAF as a matter of urgency. One means of achieving this was to launch a quite revolutionary pilot training scheme. Under this young would-be aviators were offered a Short-Service commission. Aspiring pilots would be taken on, provided they met the still stringent requirements, as 'temporary officers'. They would be retained for up to five years (with possible opportunities of further engagement) and then be returned to civilian life with a quite handsome gratuity. The graduates would never achieve the prestige and promotion prospects that Cranwell offered but it was the next best thing.

Terry jumped at this second, unexpected, chance. As Terry had passed all the necessary written and medical tests, he had little difficulty in being accepted, subject only to the usual proviso that he showed sufficient aptitude for flying. The RAF's method of determining this was to send the newcomers to a civilian training school, run under contract to the air force on military lines. Here they were given the normal ab initio RAF flying training course. If they passed this, and only if they passed this, they would be accepted into the RAF as officers with the lowest of all commissioned ranks, that of an acting pilot officer. While at their civil flying school, they were acting pilot officers on probation.

The depression which had settled on Terry was lifted. A career with the RAF had come into his sights after all. It would be up to him to see that it stayed within his sights.

The creation of the Short-Service commission scheme for pilots and the parallel build up of the Auxiliary Air Force for week-end flyers capable of handling the latest military planes were hastily improvised moves which, in all probibility, saved the country from invasion in 1940. History has shown that the majority of the pilots who fought in the Battle of Britain received their RAF training under one or other of these schemes. And as this story relates, the success of these emergency measures didn't stop there. By 1942, after three years of war, there were few of the pre-war Cranwell trained pilots left to fight. By then the RAF was being run and controlled at airfield level to a great extent by the young men who, in the late 1930s, had responded to the call when the alarm bells had rung and the cry was for the young and adventurous men to take to the air: to build up the long neglected air defences of Britain.

CHAPTER FOUR

Halcyon Days

A fit and determined acting pilot officer, on probation, Terry Bulloch reported for flying training at Prestwick Airport in November 1936. He was aged 20 and a much relieved man. At last, he was being given a chance to become an RAF pilot. The rest would be up to him. The civilian flying school which held the RAF contract was Scottish Aviation. Like other Elementary Flying Training Schools (EFTS) of the RAF, they gave initial instruction in the De Havilland DH82A, better known as the Tiger Moth. It had a 130 hp Gipsy Major engine. It was a good trainer because it was not all that easy to fly. It was a machine in which instructors could accurately sort 'the men from the boys'.

As with the other EFTS, the instructors had RAF associations. Terry found himself assigned to a Flying Officer Capper and his first flight took place on 16 November. Thanks in part to the unofficial experience he had gained at Newtownards, he had little difficulty in satisfying his instructor and, after less than six hours of dual instruction, he was soon allowed to fly solo. The chief instructor was a well-known pilot. Squadron Leader David McIntyre had earned himself the nickname of 'All-Weather Mac' because of his ability to fly under even the most appalling conditions. As was their custom, the new pupil was personally tested by All-Weather Mac before being sent off on his own for the first time.

More advanced instruction followed and, a few weeks before his 21st birthday, Terry successfully passed all necessary tests laid down by the EFTS and was declared ready to progress to bigger RAF planes. Scottish Aviation marked him only as 'Average'.

The young acting pilot officer was next posted to No 6 Flying Training School at Netheravon, Wilts. This was a real RAF station. Here he was taught to fly the much faster and bigger bi-plane, the Hawker Hart. Every pilot who flew the Hart loved it. It was snappy, fairly fast and handled beautifully. At Netheravon, he also commenced night-flying in the similar Hawker Audax. Both planes had Rolls Royce Kestrel engines of several times the power of the Tiger's Gipsy one. Now turned 21, he was taught aerobatics and began to put into practice the navigation methods which he had been taught in ground-school. This allowed Terry in his Hart to fly across the country to other RAF Stations.

In May 1937, he was officially commissioned in the RAF. By then he was looping and rolling his Hart all over the sky as he flew around Britain. The plane was a two-seater and he often shared these enjoyable flights with a fellow pupil-pilot, Acting Pilot Officer Perioli: two happy young men revelling in their increasing mastery of the skies.

Life in the RAF wasn't just flying aircraft. As a junior officer, Terry had to take part in discipline and parades (but not with his Irish Pipes or his Leader's mace!). Flying also alternated with classroom work. There, Terry learnt the rudiments of meteorology, navigation, maps and charts as well as being taught the 'ins and outs' of the plane's engine propeller and instruments.

Navigation is an art which depends much upon quickness and accuracy with figures. Maths had never been Terry's best subject but he applied himself so assiduously to the subject that he emerged from Netheravon with the course's navigation prize. He left Netheravon with an assessment of 'above average'. RAF pilots are assessed annually and this was the lowest rating that Terry, henceforth, was to receive. The only higher was the rarely given 'Exceptional'.

Terry Bulloch now faced an important decision. Students who excelled at navigation were not posted to Fighter Command. Terry found that he had a choice. He could elect to be posted to either a Bomber Command or to a Coastal Command station.

Bomber Command had a lot to offer. It was well publicised, and given priority. It flew the largest planes in the RAF and it was known that even larger ones, Wellingtons and Stirlings, would shortly be flowing into the Bomber Command Stations. By contrast, Coastal Command was almost unknown and little regarded. It was almost completely new, having been first created in 1936 after a long dispute between the RAF and the Navy as to which Service should have the responsibilities of guarding over Britain's off-shore waters. It had few planes and not such large ones. It was Cinderella to the more glamorous commands of Fighter and Bomber. Few knew what its role would be in wartime. The general impression, especially in Naval circles, was that it would serve as the 'eyes' of the Navy's battle-fleets. It had few squadrons and few airfields, almost entirely facing the North Sea.

Terry Bulloch had read more than his companions. History had been his best subject at school. He had a feeling for British history and knew that the fate of the British Isles in war depended upon its ability to maintain maritime invincibility. He was also a person who could look ahead. The newness of Coastal Command attracted, rather than repelled, him. In a new command, promotion might come faster. He wanted to be a *permanent* part of the RAF, not just a Short-Service intake. The navigation prize he had worked so hard to win, seemed to be of more use in Coastal Command. Navigation over land was, in those days, largely map-reading – a matter of being able to pinpoint the way by visual means. Planes followed railway lines and checked their position by the large towns that they overflew. Over the featureless sea, the skill of the navigator and the meteorologist were more needed.

Terry was also one of the more serious students. Many of the dashing young men who had joined alongside him were just that: dashing young men who were enjoying life to the full without too much thought to their future. Quite naturally, they opted for Fighter or Bomber Command postings with a barely a thought about poor little Cinderella. But for Terry, Coastal seemed to point the way.

For Coastal Command to have won the battle for the RAF against the Navy was one thing. To get hold of the planes to do the job was quite another. The policy in the RAF was to build up a large Fighter Command and to match this with a sizable Bomber Command. Hitler possessed many good fighters and powerful bombers and both had been tried out with success in the Spanish Civil War. Fortunately, British designers had come up with two new fighter planes which seemed a match for the German Messerschmitt and Heinkel fighters which had fought so well for Franco in Spain. Production of these two, the Hurricane and Spitfire, was being given top priority. Likewise the decision had been made to produce the Wellington, Whitley and forthcoming Stirling bombers with equal urgency.

These decisions left Coastal Command crying in the wilderness. A plan was put into action to convert the large four-engined Empire Flying boats built by Short Bros, into military planes for use by Coastal Command but the progress was slow, especially as the Stirlings wanted for Bomber Command came from the same factory.

In 1937 Coastal Command comprised a few squadrons of obsolete bi-plane torpedo bombers, the Vildebeests, and several squadrons of a plane which the RAF had ordered in large numbers but which it scarcely knew what to do with due to its several limitations.

The Avro Anson was slow. It could carry few bombs. It had no great range of action. It was a fairly large target, and yet was virtually unarmoured. Its single gun turret carried but one machine gun. Compared with the new planes coming off the assembly lines of Germany and Italy*, it was woefully inadequate. Offensively, it was fitted with one gun fixed to fire forwards. This was a ·303 machine gun quite incapable of damaging a warship. It was also difficult to imagine when this could be used as the Anson's lack of speed made it unlikely to be able to overhaul any enemy in the skies. Towards the end of the 1914-18 war, the plane used for Coastal duties was the Blackburn Kitten. It was faster and carried a larger bomb load than its replacement in the 1930s!

For all its limitations, the Anson, powered by two Armstrong Siddeley engines (Cheetah IX) of 310 hp, was a greatly loved plane. It was absolutely viceless and the simplest twin-engined to fly. No matter what a poor or hamfisted pilot did, it would flop safely onto the ground. It was also fairly rugged and totally forgiving of mishandling in the air. The fuselage was wide and commodious and could carry quite a few passengers in cold comfort. It was as lovable as a Teddy Bear – and about as hostile. The Avro Anson soon earned the nickname of 'Faithful Annie'. The choice of a female

* Italian war planes were also of advanced design and had likewise been proved in the 1935-36 Spanish Civil War.

name was inevitable. Yet it was the plane which, in 1937, formed the backbone of Coastal Command.

Having made his decision to join the new Command, Terry was posted to 220 Squadron. He had enjoyed his training at Netheravon and was becoming a name to be noted. He flew well. He had won the navigation prize. He had been assessed 'above average' and he didn't get himself into foolish scrapes. Nor was he a nuisance in the Mess, where he regularly paid his bills. It was also appreciated that he kept himself fit and played games hard. He was about to experience the joys of squadron life. He had ceased to be a 'sprog', i.e. a new pilot.

No 220 Squadron inhabited the comfortable new RAF Station of Bircham Newton. It was in Norfolk and had purposely been built close to the North Sea so as to be in a good position to be able to send planes out to look for any German ships that might be trying to break out into the Atlantic, via the North Sea (which the Germans called 'The German Ocean'). Inevitably, 220 Squadron operated Ansons. Compared with the manoeuverable Hart and Audax planes, the Anson was a 'piece of cake' to fly. If a pilot could not fly this, then he couldn't fly anything. Terry needed only the briefest of instruction before being passed to fly dear old 'Faithful Annie'.

For the next eight months, Pilot Officer Terry Bulloch (he had been able to drop the 'Acting') settled down to enjoy squadron life. To be a pilot of the RAF in those halcyon days was to enjoy the life of the gods. Terry found himself among a bunch of happy-go-lucky young men of similar age and disposition. In the main, they did not take life all that seriously but concentrated upon living it to the full with all the excess enthusiasm of fitness and youth.

Many of the young pilots shared Terry's burning desire to fly. To them, just to be a pilot was to be released, both physically and metaphorically, from all the worries and tensions of the world below. Because of the need to pass every six months the RAF's rigorous medical tests, they did not allow their excesses of spirits to affect their fitness. They lived hard but played games with equal zest. In pre-war Service life in the RAF there were only two serious crimes likely to cut short a young officer's career. By far the more serious was to get into debt and renege on their Mess account. The other crime was to bust up planes. This was 'rather a bad show'.

Being the newest of the three services, the RAF was less hidebound by tradition: less stuffy, too. Pilots, in particular, were allowed a certain lassitude with regards discipline and dress. Spit and polish had their places but not too dominant ones. Pilots were also looked upon with genuine affection by the men whose duties were to service and maintain the planes. Many had wanted to be pilots but had been found wanting. On the whole there was a good camaraderie between those who flew and those who cared for the planes. The aircraft were loved and cherished by all. It was the common bond between earthmen and skymen.

Young exuberant airmen did not always behave well. Many were apt to drive furiously about the peaceful countryside in which their airfields had been sited, in noisy sports cars with little regard to the feelings of others. With long scarves trailing behind them and, at times, with others standing on the running-boards, they shattered the peace of the English countryside.

Drinking large quantities of beer often went with the wild driving: specially at night when the pubs were open. Thanks to their quick reactions (the RAF 'Cambridge' tests were an excellent guide to these), and excellent eyesight, few serious accidents occurred. The low level of traffic in the country areas also contributed.

The general public, and even the police, were remarkably tolerant of the excesses. There was a wide-felt admiration for the young gentlemen who dared to 'go up in them there machines'. Few people had ever flown and their natural apprehension about something that was so patently unreal was heightened by the excessive amount of publicity that attended every flying accident. And, in those days, flying really was unsafe. 'You'll never get me to go up in one of those things,' was a common comment. Courage is always admired and generous allowances were made for the high spirited youths who so defied gravity.

RAF pilots were also prone to break the Rules of the Air. While aerobatics were encouraged as a means of testing one's ability to remain master of the plane under all circumstances, they had to be practised at a safe height. Unnecessary low flying and the 'beat up' at zero height of a friendly pub or a girl friend's house were definitely frowned upon. However only the more blatant and most foolhardy were severely disciplined.

The RAF held daring in some esteem and was reluctant to be too hard on those who displayed this characteristic. Yet a few lives and valuable planes were lost by such frolics. Douglas (later Sir Douglas) Bader had lost his legs through one such act of folly. At the time he was regarded as an ace pilot in the RAF and had given astonishing displays of skill and daring at the annual RAF display at Hendon.

The RAF tended to note their most dashing pilots and, to some extent, cashed in on their bravado by forming them into aerobatic formation flying teams for public displays. It was one 'return' for being allowed the great increases in RAF expenditure included in the budgets of the late 1930s.

Girls were naturally attracted by such glamorous youths with money in their pockets and sportscars in their hands. Youthful affairs sprang up but it was not the custom of the time either to marry before being in a sound financial position to do so nor to lure every girl towards the nearest bedroom. Kisses and cuddles in the backs of cars or at the cinema generally sufficed. Drug-taking was practically unknown and although most pilots smoked cigarettes or pipes, all were blissfully unaware of the associated heart or lung dangers. Doctors were equally ignorant. Only ultra keen sportsmen kept away from cigarettes.

In a Britain which was struggling to throw off the malaise which had stiffled her for so long, none typified this change of heart better than the young pilots of the RAF. Terry, while not being a prude, a tee-totaller or misogynist and still less a 'goody-goody' who curried favour by a slavish obeying of orders, was separated in part from some of the more extrovert fellow pilots by the lingering traces of his childhood shyness. Yvonne recalls that when he travelled back to Belfast for some leave, he did not eat anything during a whole day spent on trains and boats because of his reluctance to enter alone the dining saloons available. Being Ulster-Irish also made him slightly apart from the others. It was his nature to take things that mattered with seriousness. To some, he was still a 'bit of a loner'.

Hitler was becoming bolder and Mussolini more truculent. The unwillingness of either Britain or France to take decisive action had encouraged them. Italy had invaded Abyssinia and proclaimed it as part of the new Italian Empire. Mussolini was boasting that the Mediterranean, Britain's essential life-line to India and beyond, was henceforth '*Mare nostrum*' (our sea). Hitler, having seized the Saar basin from France without opposition, was steadily devouring Europe bit by bit. Austria was overrun without a shot being fired. All Europe trembled. Which country would next be seized?

As summer of 1938 advanced, Terry was selected to attend a three month long navigational course with the School of General Reconnaissance at Thorney Island, near Portsmouth. Here, in addition to being taught the finer points of navigation, he was taught how to co-operate closely with the Navy. It made a nice change from the gunnery and bombing practices and the almost endless formation flying practice that was occupying most of his flying time at Bircham Newton. It was an interesting course although Terry did not relish the thought that, for three months, he himself would not be flying the Ansons which the School used. These Ansons were 'flying classrooms' and handled by the instructors.

For all its warlike limitations, Faithful Annie made an excellent navigational trainer. It had lots of room inside. Its very slowness made it more susceptible to wind changes. They would blow it miles off track unless constantly checked and their effects countered by alterations of heading. Much of the course took place in classrooms. Terry was indoctrinated into the art of astro-navigation and practised finding a position by 'shooting' the sun, moon, stars and planets using a sextant and astro tables.

While learning these new 'tricks' at Thorney Island, Europe drifted closer to war. The Czechoslovakian crisis arose and only a much publicised climb-down by Neville Chamberlain, the British Prime Minister, prevented its outbreak. Again Hitler obtained all that he wanted without wasting a round of ammunition. The Press hailed Chamberlain as a Saviour but some saw his frantic dash to Germany for what it really was: a terrified dash by a frightened man, willing to buy peace at any price. Churchill's was one of the voices crying alarm. He was dubbed a warmonger and Britons went on enjoying the rise in prosperity that had been triggered by the decision to greatly increase military expenditure 'just in case'.

By October 1938, Terry Bulloch was back with his squadron. The atmosphere was changing. Whatever assurances came from Parliament, the RAF, including Bircham Newton, was preparing for war. 220 Squadron was preparing for the day when it might have to sally forth to locate and shadow a German battle-fleet bent on challenging the might of the Royal Navy. 220 Squadron might even have to bomb the enemy with its small quiver of light bombs. The German Navy was being increased in size and efficiency at a furious pace. It was becoming a real threat to the RN.

Nobody seems to have correctly divined what the role of Coastal would be in the war against Germany which was looming close. The Chiefs of Staff seemed content to accept that Coastal Command would be the Navy's 'advanced eyes'. Their Ansons could see well over the horizon and that seemed sufficient. The general impression that Terry had gained from his stay at Thorney Island was that the Navy was preparing to fight a battle similar to the Battle of Jutland, the battle that in 1916 prevented the German fleet from breaking out into the Atlantic where it could inflict mortal blows against British convoys. Enemy submarines appear to have been discounted. Submarines in the Royal Navy were regarded as adjuncts to the fighting surface ships. Their role was to sail alongside the battle-fleets and to torpedo enemy fighting ships. British subs – French and Italian ones also, had been designed accordingly. Many were fast and quite large. The few small German ones hardly came into the picture at all.

The cause of this complacency by a nation which had been all but starved into submission in the first world war by German submarines' destruction of Atlantic convoys, was that the British had a device which it considered would put paid to maurauding U-boats once and for all. This was Asdic, the device which, under ideal listening conditions (seldom attainable in the Atlantic) could detect the presence of an underwater craft at a range of more than a mile or two. It operated on an echo principle. Such was the Admiralty's faith in Asdic, that a public statement had been made that, 'Never again would Britain be threatened by underwater craft'. Asdic had been fitted to Naval destroyers. That, they assumed, was the end of any U-boat threat.

One consequence of this mistaken belief was that Coastal Command carried out no anti-submarine training even though war was clearly close at hand. Neither did Coastal Command possess, apart from one squadron of Sunderland flying boats, any modern plane capable of carrying out the long patrols over the oceans that would be necessary to detect any U-boats in the Atlantic. Nor were there any Coastal Command bases near to the shores of the Atlantic, except for one in Cornwall. The emphasis in Coastal Command was on the North Sea and it was over these waters that 220 Squadron so assiduously practised their exercises.

A diversion from their usual routine came about when on 21 March the squadron was ordered to provide an escort across the Channel to the plane carrying the French President, Monsieur Lebrun, to London on a formal visit. Fifteen Ansons, flying in good formation, carried out the task and repeated the performance a few days later when he returned. Whether the visitor was impressed is not known. A politician with no military knowledge might have been but one with only a hazy idea of planes would have had doubts. Presumably this was meant as a display of might. If this was so, then why use such slow and cumbersome aircraft? Were these 'sitting ducks' the best that Britain could muster?

On the credit side, as talk of war became more open, exercises that involved close co-operation with the Navy increased. These included passing messages between ships and planes by flash-lamp and wireless. Terry and the others became familiar with both RAF and RN coding procedures and codes. This was to ensure that if any plane were to sight a German battle-fleet trying to traverse the North Sea, the news of the sighting could be instantly relayed to the Admiralty. Communications had gone sadly wrong during the Battle of Jutland and the Admiralty was taking care that its 'advanced eyes' would be in a position to provide the correct information without delay.

Pilot Officer Bulloch was becoming a name to note in the squadron. He had been ordered to take part in both the formation flights which 'guarded' the French PM. In bombing exercises, he established a reputation of being 'a dead-eyed Dick'. The Anson (typically!) carried no bombsight and bombs had to be dropped by the pilot simply by eye. He was regarded as a first-class navigator. He had passed his GR course and was recognised as one of the surest pilots in the unit. It was typical of his thoroughness that, on every bombing exercise, he recorded the found errors in his neatly kept log book. Bearing in mind that he was dropping solely by eye,

(Left) At Netheravon, 1937. *(Right)* Faithful Annies of A Flight, 220 Squadron.

A Flight, 220 Squadron, Christmas 1937. Terry Bulloch is second from the left.

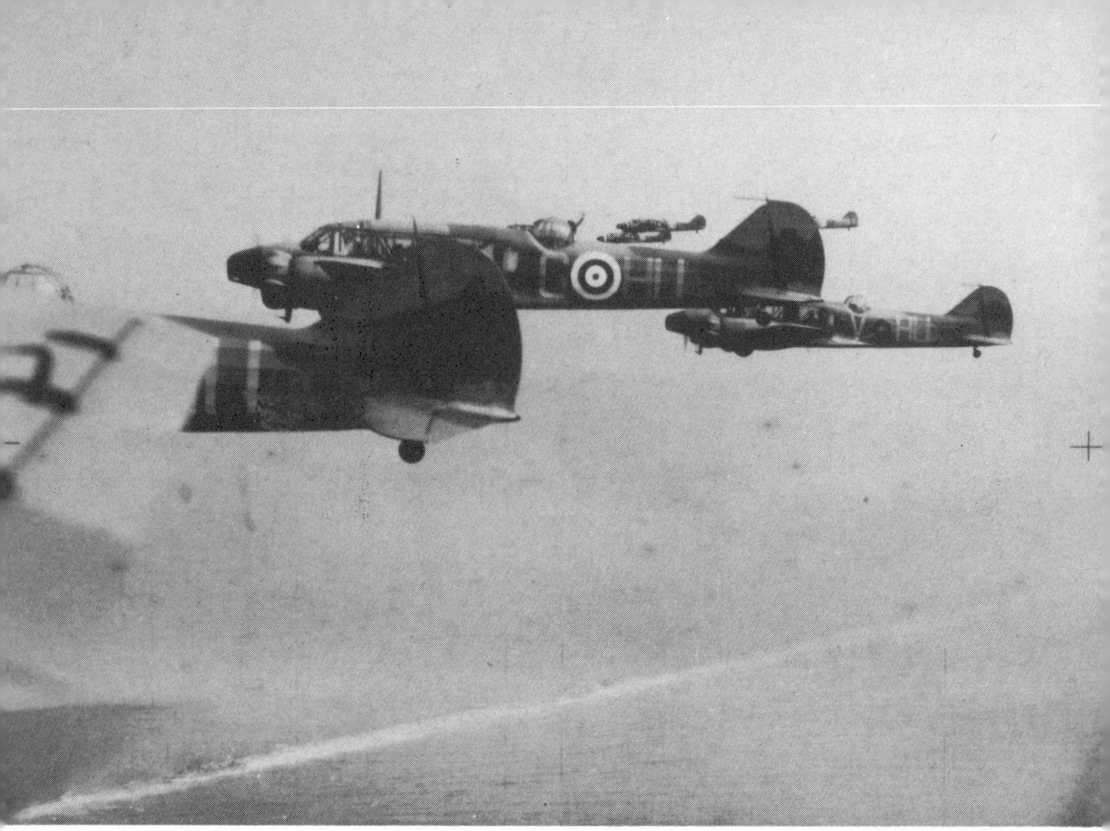

No 220 Squadron escorting the French President (Monsieur Lebrun) from Calais to Dover, 21st March, 1939.

C Flight, 206 Squadron, Bircham Newton. Terry is fifth from the left.

the errors of 50 feet or less recorded are impressive. All in all, he had found his metier and was making his mark.

In his enthusiasm, Terry also made another mark: one that almost resulted in his dismissal from the Service. As co-operation between the two Services increased, the squadron occasionally found itself exercising with the Home Fleet. To locate, shadow and report upon the Home fleet on manoeuvres was excellent practice for the role expected of the squadron in wartime. On one such occasion, Terry was sent out to track down a battleship force headed by HMS *Nelson*, at that time the most powerful battleship in the Navy.

True to form, Terry located his target and, to emphasise the point, came diving out of the clouds and planted an aluminium sea-marker slap on the great ship's massive foredeck. It made quite a mess. However the Navy did not seem to appreciate this excellent piece of low-level bombing and Terry found himself on the mat. To assuage the wrath of the Admirals, Terry had to be officially reprimanded. It is possible, however, that those in HQ who were sensibly looking ahead for men to lead the Command into battle might have noted the action with secret approbation. Pilot Officer Bulloch clearly had the right spirit: was obviously proud of his unit and the accuracy of the 'bomb' hit confirmed his skill.

It seems possible that the *Nelson* incident may even have resulted in having a further tick put against his name. Almost at once he was promoted to Flying Officer.

In the USA, in 1921 Captain Billy Mitchell of the US Army Air Corps, had gone one further. Determined to prove the superiority of air power, he requested permission to carry out a series of bombing attacks on former German warships, culminating in the battleship *Ostfriesland*. However, firmly believing that, contrary to the Navy's view, planes *could* sink ships, he disregarded the conditions laid down for carefully controlled timed hits. He proved his point; he sank his target, with continual bombardments and heavy bombs; he was later dismissed the Service for similar disregarding of orders, but was restored and rose to become a famous fighting general. In addition, the USA's most successful medium bomber of World War II was named after him. The Mitchell (B25) ensured that none would ever forget that planes could sink capital ships. The Bullochs and Mitchells of this world are not always appreciated, especially during sleeping years of peace, but they come into their own when the chips are down.

As well as being promoted, Terry was also made an instructor. He was clearly on his way up.

Another change from the usual routine of bombing, photography and communication exercises, involved rather mysterious exercises that were carried out in conjunction with the Bawdsey Research Station – a unit about which Terry and his brother pilots knew nothing. They had no idea what was involved. All they had to do was to fly certain tracks off the coast for no apparent purpose. Yet these were vitally important flights. The apparatus being tested by the Bawdsey Research Station was to become Radar – the war-winning weapon which soon was to enable Fighter Command to detect enemy planes before they reached our coasts. Radar later was fitted to aircraft of Coastal Command to help find enemy ships. When so fitted, it was known as Air to Surface Vessel (ASV). The device was classified as Top Secret and the secret was well kept.

As the RAF expanded, new squadrons of Coastal Command were formed. At the outbreak of war there were 16, nearly all equipped with Ansons. Better planes were on the way. In their haste to build up Bomber and Fighting Commands that could match the Luftwaffe of Hermann Goering, the re-equipment of Coastal Command was left to others. Eyes were turned overseas. In USA Lockheeds had produced a swift and reliable small airliner, the Lockheed 10 (Electra). It handled with the aplomb of a military plane. A military version was being planned and a large order from Britain was placed, literally 'off the drawing-board'. These would be assigned to Coastal Command. In its new guise, the Lockheed 10 was to be called the Hudson. It was to be the Fairy Godmother that Cinderella much needed.

A few Hudsons were brought across on the decks of merchant ships and to increase the numbers, a new aircraft factory-one of the so-called shadow factories, was hastily built on the edge of Speke civil airfield, Liverpool, to assemble Hudsons from parts brought across from the New World. This was but one sign that Britain was awakening.

As Terry flew across England on various exercises (pilots of 220 used frequently to visit other stations within the Command) he could see for himself the vast new works that were being carried out. Huge new underground fuel (petrol) storage tanks were being excavated. New RAF stations were being built close to the East Coast; both for Bomber and Coastal Commands. Hawkers and Vickers were working flat out to produce the Hurricanes, Spitfires (from Vicker's subsidiary Supermarines) and Wellingtons. Handley Page was tooling up for a huge supply of Hampden medium bombers and Bristols were completing a large order for the Blenheim light bomber.

Bircham Newton, itself, was being equipped with underground petrol storage tanks. The shipyards were humming with new orders. Taxation to pay for these new arms reached record levels but the people on the whole cheered, rather than decried, this measure. The Lion had had its tail twisted too often. The pacifists in Parliament had reigned for too long.

As the last summer of peace, the summer of 1939, droned on with glorious weather and great sporting results (England regained the Ashes and an Englishman, Henry Cotton, broke the Americans' stranglehold over our Golf Open), Terry and his fellow pilots of 220 Squadron found themselves flying more frequently. Gone were the restrictions which earlier had compelled the RAF to limit their hours in the air. The increased spending allowed by the larger budgets had ended the period of fuel economy. In preparation for what would have to be done in wartime, Terry had learnt his way around all the major RAF Stations, which now covered the East Coast. His exercises also had taught him to recognise the coastline and lightships of Belgium and Holland as well as those of Eastern England.

In the classrooms he had become adroit at ship recognition: both British and those of the potential enemies. The present backbone of the German Navy were their two new battlecruisers, *Scharnhorst* and *Gneisenau*. They were backed up by a few modern cruisers and three so-called 'pocket battleships'. Terry had to be sure of the outlines of all types in order to be able to report upon them accurately.

Aerial photography was another skill that the squadron practised. As best they could in their outmoded Avro Ansons, the pilots of 220 Squadron were prepared to play their part as 'the eyes of the British fleet'.

A week or two before that fateful 3 September 1939 when Britain and Germany were to be at war again (21 years after the cessation of the 'war to end all wars'), one of Coastal Command's new American-built Lockheed Hudsons visited Bircham Newton. Terry was one of the pilots who managed to get a flight in it. It impressed him greatly. It made Faithful Annie seem her age.

He had also been asked to carry out a completely new exercise. This was to fly around a convoy. The Chiefs of Staff were now so certain that war had become inevitable that they had ordered the ships which plied up and down the North Sea to form themselves into convoys: the first to be formed since 1918. Terry duly located the convoy and flew around it. It was a strange exercise: 'Anti-submarine', they called it but if it had been 'for real' there was little that Faithful Annie could have done to any enemy submarine found on the surface.

In all, Terry had flown over 700 hours yet it was the first occasion that either he, or his Coastal Command squadron, had concerned themselves with submarines.

Two weeks of leave were due to him. Scarcely had he reached home when he was recalled. Hitler had marched into Poland. Britain had issued ultimatums to Germany to withdraw. By then Hitler had lost all fear of Britain which for years had used big words but had kept its fist closed.

By 11 o'clock on 3 September Terry Bulloch was at war with Nazi Germany: in the 'front line', in command of his friendly Anson. He knew not what to expect but he was not afraid.

CHAPTER FIVE

A Score to Settle

The reality of war came as a profound shock to the British people and especially to the pilots of the RAF who knew that they would be immediately involved at the sharpest point of action: in the air slugging it out with the formidable Luftwaffe. The fact that war had been expected did little to cushion the shock. To train for war was very different from being an active participant. Lifeboat drill at sea is not the same as having to abandon ship.

The first few days of war seemed totally unreal. War had been something that filled history books: a remote subject where terrible tragedies happened to other people: where heroic deeds were performed. War had, it was believed, been outlawed by the 1914-18 conflict, the 'War to end all wars'.

After the initial shock had worn off; after the pleasant surprise at discovering that Britain was not being blasted by a rain of German bombs, as had been widely forecast, it began to be realised that little had happened to change the pattern of life for the pilots of 220 Squadron. Terry and his fellow pilots not only came to accept the new experience but to enjoy the war. The absence of the expected bombing itself was a relief. Also, being at war added an extra dimension to every flight. To carry out exercises over the North Sea had always been a pleasure, rather than a chore, for Terry but to do so when at any time an enemy plane or ship might be spotted, added an edge that was many times more exhilarating. It put him on his mettle. Another edge that Terry had over others was that, while millions were rushing to join up, he was well ahead, in position and almost a key piece on a gigantic chessboard.

Throughout the period of the 'phoney war' – a period which lasted from September 1939 up to April 1940 – the war for many RAF pilots seemed little more than a game: albeit a deadly dangerous one. Youth relishes danger. Youth looks for a challenge. Youth has surplus energy to burn. The war satisfied all these wants without, so it seemed, much likelihood of being personally involved in pain or suffering.

Flying required the same skills and judgements that had been called for on the playing fields at school. Guts and a bit of cunning were required to beat the other chap or else he beat you and that was a 'poor show'. It let the side down and that would never do. The RAF selection boards had been wise to give credit to those who had excelled at games. By selecting Terry and others like him, they had chosen well. More staid and bookish types would have served equally well in peacetime but not in war.

In a plane, a pilot not only is able to regard each war sortie as another demanding 'game' but also as a strictly impersonal one. He never comes into personal contact with the enemy. He seldom sees the people whom he is trying so hard to kill. Likewise he remains invisible to them. The sights and smells of the blood and guts of his enemies, even the sounds of his own bombs dropping, remain outside his perception. The contest is a simple one: 'Can I get this complicated piece of machinery into the right place at the right time?' 'Can I, by luck or judgement get away Scot free?' 'Do I kill him or he me?'

An airman, as opposed to a soldier, is on his own. He is not weighed down by orders that, to him, make no sense. He is not an insignificant cog in a giant machine beyond his comprehension. He fights an individual battle. He is his own commander with no superior in sight. It has rightly been said that 'A captain of an aircraft is the nearest thing to an absolute monarch, in the twentieth century.'

Life at Bircham Newton remained remarkably unaltered. The Mess still served excellent food although the number of mouths rapidly grew. The airfield became better guarded, with a few soldiers and sandbags visible at strategic points. A strictly enforced blackout became a daily chore and some windows were covered with a lattice of protective strips. Petrol was rationed and its limitation imposed restrictions on off-duty activities. It also became 'more dicey' to drive at night as all headlights had to be doused and masked.

Officers were issued with service revolvers although aircrew could hardly imagine how they could be of use to them. Gas masks had to be carried at all times. Poison gas was something that everyone feared, consequently gas-drills were taken seriously. Fortunately, Britain had ample stocks of this horrible weapon and the Germans knew it. The deterrent was sufficient and neither side resorted to its use.

Outside the camp, conditions were equally unreal. The war which had been on people's minds for years was proving to be far less dreadful than most had imagined. There was tremendous relief that Britain was not being bombed. In anticipation of the cities being attacked from above, children had been parted from their parents and sent into the safety of the countryside, far distant from the East Coast. Slit trenches had been dug in every town and village and air-raid shelters put up on a massive scale. A Government-inspired design, the Anderson shelter, was readily available. Citizens dutifully carried their gas-masks everywhere and from John O' Groats to Land's End householders had contrived effective black-out curtains. Wardens patrolled the streets at night to ensure that no chink of light appeared over Britain: no guidance for the dreaded bombers of the enemy: not that any attempted to attack.

Food rationing during the period of the 'phoney war' was not severe. Chocolate and other sweets were still available. Restaurants and pubs flourished. Occasionally, specific brands of beer or Scotch would be in short supply and there was a general belief that the beer was more watered.

Pubs in particular did a roaring trade. About half the population soon found itself living away from home: in a new job, in one of the Services, in camps or just being shuffled about as Britons adjusted to the change of circumstances. Pubs were the form of recreation which made the changes worthwhile. With their blackout and massive overcrowding, they developed some glorious fugs. The many new thick uniforms of the troops, wardens, Land Army girls etc added to the heavy atmosphere. Cigarettes were not too hard to get and the entire population seemed to have taken to the habit. Their smoke also added to the sweaty confusion. The wholesale relief that the country was not being bombed found expression in the beery songs that filled the saloons and bars. Songs like 'Roll out the Barrel' and 'We're going to hang out our washing on the

Siegfried Line ...*' were boisterously bawled by the beery crowds. War, far from being almost too horrible to contemplate, was turning out to be great fun.

While Britons celebrated their initial war experiences, Hitler's efficient war machine rapidly smashed Poland to smithereens. Stalin, with whom Hitler had formed a surprising alliance, completed the Polish massacre, by seizing the east half of that unhappy country. Britain and France, who had declared war on Germany because of her invasion of Poland, still backed away from the inevitable. France stood behind her chain of forts – the Maginot Line. Britain sent troops to France, a small but much publicised British Expeditionary Force, to stand beside her ally.

The RAF did make an attempt to attack German shipping but the daylight raids on the German ports proved so expensive of men and planes (Wellingtons) that they were soon stopped. The German fighters – the redoubtable Me109s to the fore – shot the Wellingtons out of the sky. Also, Britons were not geared psychologically for the kind of total war that Hitler had begun. When one or two Wellingtons did reach the Kiel Canal, which the Navy wanted blocked and destroyed, in order to deny German ships in the Baltic easy access to the North Sea, the pilots did not drop their bombs because they sighted men and women in the vicinity! It was beyond their sense of decency to risk harming civilians. Later, of course, under 'Bomber' Harris, the same Bomber Command rained thousands of tons of bombs on every major German city, regardless of the fate of the civilians below.

As well as these abortive and disastrous early attacks, the RAF used Bomber Command to fly over Germany at night and to drop leaflets urging the population to turn against Hitler and so stop the war by internal political means. The chances of the Germans agreeing to quit so tamely, after all the successes achieved in Poland, were minimal but the policy and the raids continued for the whole of that first unreal winter of war.

Only at sea had Britain's war begun in earnest. Admiral Doenitz had prepared in advance for war with Britain and France and, although only having a small force of U-boats, had arranged for

---

* The Siegfried Line was a chain of forts built by the Germans to protect their West flank from attack by France.

them to be at sea in attacking positions. His smaller boats were in the North Sea and his 22/23 larger ones were out in the Atlantic or preparing to journey there. From 3 September onwards, they began to sink Allied ships at an alarming rate. Passenger ships, merchant ships, naval vessels, big and small, were all sent to the bottom. One ace U-boat commander, Günther Prien, penetrated the Navy's Home Fleet base at Scapa Flow and sank the battleship *Royal Oak*. The *Courageous*, one of the Navy's few aircraft carriers, was also sunk and the latest carrier, the *Ark Royal*, would also have suffered a similar fate, but for the faulty torpedoes narrowly missing her.

Asdic did nothing to stop the killing, although ships were being put into convoys and protected by naval craft fitted with this device. Worse still, a few of Germany's modern ships, including their vaunted 'pocket battleships' did manage to break out into the Atlantic and were sinking ships at will. Long-range German aircraft, their Focke-Wulf Condors, joined in the killing and for some months their successes were the equal of the U-boats'.

Against this background, life for Terry Bulloch and the rest of 220 Squadron went largely unchanged. In Terry's RAF log book is written in red in large letters 'WAR DECLARED AGAINST GERMANY 1100 HOURS 3/9/39.' He, at least, had been expecting dramatic developments.

Not for three days, however, was he ordered to fly at all. And when he did again take to the air, it was only to complete another exercise with the 'Bawdsey Research Station', not that he or anyone else in the unit, knew what it was. Thereafter the exercises continued much as they had done in peacetime, although never again was he asked to practise formation flying. This much-loved exercise had now been deleted. For years the RAF seems to have been almost obsessed by this form of training, only to drop the practice when the real thing came.

A more interesting change in the curriculum was that the new 'anti-submarine' exercise began to occur with regularity. Coastal Command was awakening to its role in wartime. Another new task for the squadron was to search for German mines. The enemy had sprung a successful surprise. They had invented a new form of mine, one that was triggered by the passing of the metal hull of any ship overhead – the so-called Magnetic Mine. U-boats and other small craft had spread these over a wide area of the North Sea and they caused heavy casualties among the ships that plied along the East

Coast. Fortunately, the Navy was swift to find the remedy. This was to de-gauss (demagnify) all ships. But it took time and in the meanwhile shipping losses from this new form of warfare added to the problems at sea.

Another new form of exercise for Terry and his colleagues was: 'co-operating with aerodrome defence unit'. The soldiers in their newly dug trenches needed to practise detecting planes and swinging their guns to bear on the targets.

For all these changes to their flying routine, the seriousness of war gradually diminished. By the end of September, with Poland shattered, even the land fighting in Europe ceased. The world was at war but, apart from the events at sea, scarcely a shot was being fired.

The state of 'frightfulness' of that first month of war is well illustrated by an entry in Terry's log book on 25 September: 'Joy rides for defence unit'. That could hardly have been contemplated three weeks earlier when he and the rest of the pilots had listened, with bated breath, to Neville Chamberlain proclaiming over the wireless that we were at war with Germany and when, only minutes later, the sirens all over Britain had sounded in earnest for the first time, that celebrated false alarm, still remembered for the shivers up the spine that were felt by all who heard that first wailing of war.

Patrols over the North Sea were now made with full tanks and Terry once managed to spin one out for as long as five hours. The techniques which he later developed to increase the duration of sorties had begun. These searches into the North Sea also included quite a few 'scares'. From time to time, the Admiralty considered that German capital ships might be at sea and lost no time in ordering maximum search efforts by Coastal Command: their 'advanced eyes'. All these alarms proved to be negative but even the thought that a huge enemy warship might be encountered added zest to otherwise routine patrols.

The only hostile engagement experienced during the station's first four months of World War II occurred during a period when Terry had been temporarily 'grounded' to carry out a spell of administrative duties. He was still at Bircham Newton but had been detached from 220 Squadron and assigned to Station HQ Unit. Hanging about a station HQ was never Terry's idea at the best of times and certainly not his notion of how to fight a war. Accordingly, when a call came to send another Anson on an extra North Sea patrol, he and a senior officer, Tim Vickers, who was also twiddling his thumbs at HQ, decided to answer it themselves: and to hell with their Admin duties!

The two pilots in their Anson, while cruising off the Dutch coast were surprised, literally, by being attacked by a German reconnaissance float-plane, a Heinkel 115. It fired at them as it shot past. They were not hit and at once tried to counter. However, try as they did with the Anson vibrating at top speed with throttles wide open, the float-plane rapidly disappeared ahead. Poor Faithful Annie, she couldn't even catch up her opposite number – a float-plane designed for reconnaissance rather than for speed.

The attack was a talking point back at Bircham Newton. An enemy plane had been sighted. Shots had been exchanged. The war was becoming serious!

However the war was soon to hit Terry hard. One morning in December the CO sent for him. He had bad news. Wellingtons from Bomber Command had carried out a raid on Heligoland Bight. They had been shot up. One of the persons 'missing believed killed' was Flying Officer H.L. McL. Bulloch* – his brother Larmor. In quick time, Terry borrowed the station's light aircraft – a Miles Magister – and was on his way to Mildenhall, the Bomber Command base where his brother had been stationed. He wanted to check the facts.

It was all too true. Larmor had been shot down and almost certainly killed. The kindly elder brother who had been such a lynch-pin during all Terry's early life was no more. All of a sudden, he was terribly alone. In good times or bad, Larmor had been there. Now he was gone.

Worse was to follow. Larmor had married shortly before war had been declared and Terry had not had an opportunity to meet his sister-in-law. She, also, was at Mildenhall and utterly distraught. Terry had never seen a person in such straits. It shattered him. He had never before seen a woman cry with grief. It was a meeting and sight that he was never to forget. It instilled in him a burning hatred of the Germans who had caused so much pain and agony. Nothing

* After a brief career in the Army, Larmor had transferred to the RAF and, like his younger brother, had become a pilot. Unlike Terry he had joined Bomber Command.

that he could do or say seemed the slightest comfort to Barbara. He had seldom been at ease with the opposite sex. For once in his life he was faced with a situation that left him powerless and speechless. It was the kind of situation that Larmor would have handled with tact and skill. From force of habit, he looked to him for help. The unthinkable had happened. He was on his own. Larmor could not help, now or ever again.

The same day Terry flew himself back to Bircham Newton. He had become a changed man. He was a man with a mission and with the determination to carry it out. He was out to make those bastard Germans pay for what they had done to his family and to his gentle brother. The enemy had better look out. He had a score to settle.

CHAPTER SIX

The Year of Survival 1940

Much has been written about the events that shook the world during the months of April and May 1940. Denmark was over-run, Norway invaded and Oslo taken and the fight for the rest of Norway was on. On 10 May, Germany began its astonishing advance through the Low Countries and the Ardennes by passing the Maginot Line, thought to be impregnable, and driving back the French and British armies to the Channel ports. The evacuation of the British Expeditionary Forces, together with some of the French, from the beaches of Dunkirk, followed, 350,000 men in all. Within two weeks Paris had fallen; within three the French had surrendered. At home, Neville Chamberlain, whose cry had been 'peace for our time', resigned on 10 May and a government of National unity was established, under 66-year-old Winston Churchill. Europe had been turned upside down and none knew what the future held.

Until 5th April Terry Bulloch had been at Boscombe Down, the RAF's main experimental station, on a short course to learn beam and 'blind' flying: first in the Link Trainer affixed to the classroom floor and then in the Station's Ansons with the real beam.

Upon his return to Bircham Newton, having passed the Beam Course without difficulty, he was posted from 220 to 206 Squadron. Not that the posting changed his life. Both squadrons were based at Bircham Newton and both, basically, flew Ansons. The RAF was expanding fast and the more skilful and experienced pilots were being spread around.

With Denmark fallen and Norway over-run, Terry and his new squadron stepped up the numbers of North Sea patrols. The Command had, at last, found its true niche in the war and gave almost continuous cover to the convoys of small ships which operated between the various East Coast ports. There was nothing else that Faithful Annie could do. By no stretch of imagination could she be thrown against the might of the Luftwaffe which, like the German land armies, was shortly to carry all before it in the skies on the other side of the Channel; as the RAF light bombers – Fairey Battles and Blenheims – were to find out at terrible cost.

Fortunately U-boats continued to dive at first sight of *any* RAF aircraft and although no U-boats were sighted, the probability was that any which might have been lurking, would have been put off from making any attack. Certainly the Anson, with its four small bombs was most unlikely to sink the ultra strongly built U-boats. In late May, Terry, who had flown over 100 hours during the latter parts of April, was at last able to get his hands on a Hudson. Bit by bit, 206 Squadron was being re-equipped. Faithful Annie was being phased out.

Terry spent late May and early June at Silloth in the Solway Firth. The Hudson was as modern as the Anson was not. It was like switching from an Austin 7 to a Ferrari. Whereas a couple of 'circuits and bumps' had been all that Terry had needed when being converted from the Hart to the Anson – the first twin-engined aircraft he had been asked to fly, it required a quite lengthy course to become au fait with the Hudson and its many new systems and devices. Coastal Command, which had every reason to make sure that none of their precious new Hudsons would be lost unnecessarily, had set up a special conversion unit far from the battlefield in distant Cumberland.

Among the new devices fitted to the Hudson, was the top secret ASV Mark I – the first form of radar fitted to an RAF plane. As part of the thorough conversion course, Terry took his new plane to RAF Station, St Athan, in Wales, which was where the radar experts were developing operational use of ASV. However the top secret nature of the device resulted in little instruction being given!

On his return to Bircham Newton on 9th June, Terry found himself, for the first time since war had been declared, at the sharp end of the action. The Dunkirk evacuation and the Battle of Britain which began in July, received massive daily publicity, but another equally vital battle was being fought by other units of the RAF. This one received almost no publicity. In preparation for their cross-channel invasion, code-name Operation Sealion, the Germans were massing invasion barges in every port accessible to Britain's south and east coasts. The light bombers of the RAF had orders to attack these ports and to destroy every form of shipping that might be of use to an invading army. The losses suffered during these low-level attacks against enemy shipping and their heavily defended ports were among the highest suffered by the RAF during the entire war. By war's end Coastal Command had lost over 850 aircraft on such sorties.*

The Hudson, the converted Lockheed airliner, was never intended to be used as a low-level bomber but with the Germans within sight of Britain and with their ports crammed with invasion barges, everything that the country could use to thwart their plans had to be thrown into the battle. On 12 June, flying Hudson P5162, Terry was detailed to carry out a dive-bomb attack on Boulogne Harbour. It was an indication of how swiftly events had turned. Only a few weeks before when departing for Silloth, Boulogne had been in Allied hands. It was also an unusual way of familiarising a pilot with a new type of aircraft! While the Battle of Britain was gathering in intensity other attacks followed: some made at high level and some at mast height. Ports in Germany and those they had occupied were bombed; destroyers were attacked, merchant ships attacked wherever found. Enemy airfields behind the ports were bombed both by day and night. All the practice bombing exercises which Terry had taken so seriously in Faithful Annie were now proving their worth.

In between these devastating raids upon the gathering German invasion forces, he flew an almost daily North Sea patrol, ever on the look-out for German warships heading for the Atlantic where the U-boats and the Focke-Wulf Condors were causing such carnage.

Losses among the crews carrying out near suicide attacks on German ports and airfields were heavy and on several occasions Terry's mission would be to search the seas for signs of wreckage or for possible survivors who might have been able to take to their dinghies after their plane had been shot down. The loss of fellow pilots did not affect morale. For one thing at a large station like Bircham Newton, there was a constant coming-and-going of aircrew. Some were being rested by a spell of instruction at the airfields behind the front line. Others would be sent on special

---

* By war's end, this unheralded Command had lost, in all, 2060 aircraft and sustained over 10,000 aircrew casualties.

courses. Some might be temporarily absent sick. The Service was expanding so fast that changes in personnel were almost constant. Whether a fellow pilot had been posted or had been killed seemed scarcely relevant. He was just another absent face. Also, Terry was so busy flying virtually every day and often more than once, that he scarcely had time to note whose face was missing in the Mess. Subconsciously, pilots avoided close friendships; this avoided undue suffering or grieving for lost friends. A peculiar self-deception was practised. A pilot was never killed by the enemy. The language used was that he 'had killed himself'. 'Poor old so-and-so, killed himself over Bremen.' The implication was that he had made some error: that it was his own fault – the corollary being that if you made no error, then you would survive.

If there was a lull in the fighting, pilots did not sit in the Mess and brood about lost companions. They took themselves to the nearest local. There an RAF pilot with wings on his tunic was sure of a good welcome. There he usually got himself well blotto. Even the thin wartime beer, if consumed in sufficient quantities, could blot out unpleasant memories.

A particular highlight for Terry Bulloch that momentous summer were his engagements with enemy aircraft. Flying daily within sight of enemy-held territory was almost bound to lead to such actions. The first engagement came with the early light of dawn on 28 August. It was quite usual to take-off in the dark so as to arrive at the enemy's coast at first light. It was a good way of finding out what he was up to that day. With his keen sight, Terry spotted a Heinkel 115, the same type of floatplane that had shot past him in Faithful Annie. This time their roles were reversed. A Hudson could out-fly a Heinkel in all respects. Terry was able to bring his aircraft in position for a stern attack. The Heinkel appeared to be unaware of the Hudson but soon after Terry had opened up with his front guns, the Heinkel's rear gunner returned the fire. Terry was the more accurate and almost at once the gunner disappeared, apparently hit. He left his gun dangling over the side. With the return fire silenced, Terry could then rake the enemy from stem to stern. The Heinkel pilot had but one thought: to get his plane down to the sea before it was shot down and he hastily dived towards the surface of the water and splashed his plane on to it.

Hudson of 206 Squadron, Bircham Newton. The squadron converted to Hudsons in 1940.

(Left) At Silloth in May 1940. (Right) En route to Silloth.

(Above) The B-17C Flying Fortress.

(Left) Inside the Flying Fortress.

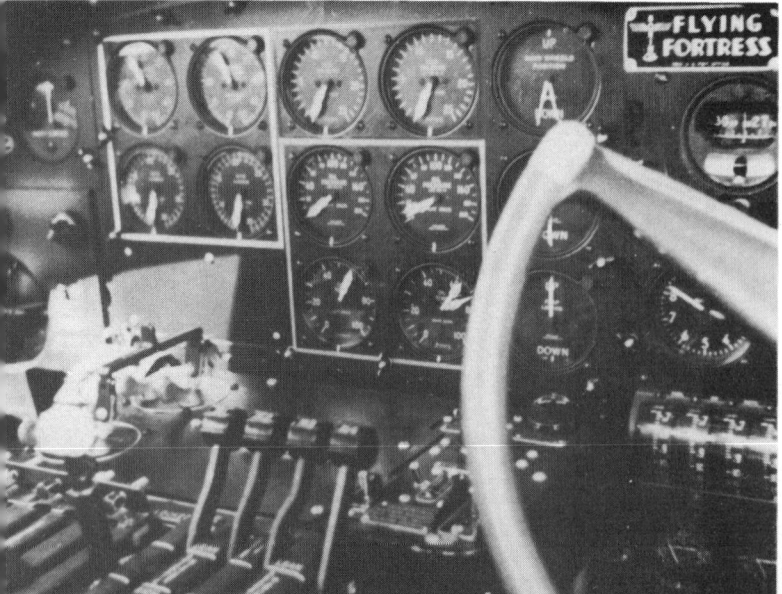

By this time the contest had strayed almost over Ijmuiden harbour which was ringed with guns. Also it was becoming lighter every moment. Terry was convinced that the Heinkel had been badly damaged with its crew wounded or killed. He was content to leave it at that. His orders were to carry out a reconnaissance of the enemy's shoreline. If he stayed where he was he would be bound to become a target not only for the shore gunners but for the Messerschmitts which would soon be brought into the fight. It was a good start to the day; one Heinkel put out of action.

A satisfactory feature of the attack was that Terry had on board his Hudson, N7275, a Royal Navy observer, a Lieutenant Poland. There was always a friendly rivalry between the two services, especially in Coastal Command over which the navy had operational control. To have blasted a Heinkel out of the sky with a Navy man onboard was something worth crowing about. It helped to kill the myth, created at Dunkirk, that the RAF had left the Navy in the lurch. The trouble there had been that the little armada of ships which were so gallantly ferrying the BEF and the Frenchmen across the Channel seldom if ever saw planes of the RAF. Instead they saw much too much of the Stuka – the German Ju87 dive-bomber. Generally the RAF was jousting with the Luftwaffe fighters at higher levels out of sight.

That same afternoon, Terry was flying again. There was no let-up during this critical time.

On 30 August, rather to his surprise, Terry was ordered to take his Hudson, T9331 loaded with Station personnel, to Aldergrove, the RAF airfield close to Belfast and Terry's home. The losses of ships by U-boats in the approaches to the ports of the Clyde and Mersey, was causing grave concern to those, like Churchill, who were far-sighted enough even during the heat of the Battle of Britain to realise that Britain's ability to carry on the war depended on supplies across the Atlantic. The south coast ports could no longer be used with the Germans so close across the Channel. Virtually all supplies had to reach Britain via the narrow North Channel between Ireland and Scotland.

Doenitz, always an astute tactician, had also grasped the same point and had concentrated his U-boats in the approaches to this North Channel. Britain had lost many destroyers and similar ships both during the unsuccessful Narvik campaign (Norway) and during the evacuation of British and French troops from France. As a result the convoys had far too few escort ships. Coastal Command had been called in to lend a helping hand.

At Aldergrove, a detachment of 206 joined other Coastal Command units carrying out Atlantic convoy escort duties. The Hudson could reach convoys several hundred miles into the Atlantic. It was capable of sinking a U-boat. It could also see off the big (ex-airliner) Focke-Wulf Condors which were proving to be almost as big a menace to the ships approaching Britain, as were the notorious U-boats. All this made sense to Terry and his fellow pilots and they began to fly patrols deep into the Atlantic to bring help to the much threatened convoys. However, they soon learnt *not* to fly over or too close to any naval vessel.

The successes gained by the Condors had made the Navy very trigger-happy. They had scarcely ever seen an RAF plane over their ships. They had seen too many of the enemy's. Consequently they had adopted the habit of blazing away at every plane. 'We shoot first and ask questions later.'

ASV Mark I, undeveloped as it was, came into its own on these patrols. It lacked the finesse and sensitivity required for the delicate task of locating U-boats, as it had been designed to do, but it had sufficient range and power to pick up targets as big as the convoys. Overwater navigation had not been brought to a fine art, although a few pilots like Terry Bulloch were skilled at it. Without ASV, it is doubtful if convoys could have been located. ASV also warned the returning pilots when land was ahead and prevented them from flying into the high ground characteristic of both Northern Ireland and the Scottish Islands.

The chance of being able to get to see his family was welcomed and Terry found the new patrols challenging and demanding. He settled into the routine swiftly. However, in the mysterious way that all wars are fought, no sooner had the detachment become au fait with its new role, than the order was countermanded. Back they all went to Bircham Newton, on 6 September. Their's not to reason why. Their's but to do and die.

That same day, Terry was detailed to carry out a dusk sweep of an area of the North Sea where enemy shipping was thought to be lurking. There was this constant fear that surface raiders might be able to sneak their way into the Atlantic: a fear heightened by the knowledge that, with Norwegian coasts under their control, it was much easier to do than had been the case earlier in the war.

Flying at 500 feet about 90 miles NE of Cromer, Terry's ever searching eyes spotted another Heinkel. He knew their outline well by then. As before, he manoeuvered his aircraft for a stern attack and fired his front guns until all their ammunition was spent. The return fire from the Heinkel's rear gun position, hit the Hudson with a very audible explosion. Terry chose to ignore this and was pleased when all return fire ceased and the Heinkel's gunner disappeared from view: was he wounded or killed? It was impossible to tell. As before, when raked with fire from behind, the Heinkel pilot dived for the sea and splashed onto it in undignified haste. Terry's gunner* was a crewman he held in high regard. Sergeant Coldbeck liberally plastered the enemy which was now on the water listing to starboard and trailing an oil slick. However, as it was still (just) afloat Terry decided to use the bombs he was carrying in case he found enemy ships. He had always enjoyed low-level bombing by eye. On his first run he dropped two of his 250lbs bombs. Another fly past showed that the Heinkel was still just afloat. A second bombing attack was made and when the Hudson departed it could be seen that the enemy was sinking fast. By then darkness had fallen so, with other areas to search (using ASV), Terry flew on.

Only then was the hit on the Hudson's nose examined. It turned out to be no hit at all. It transpired that one of the incendiary bullets fired by his own front guns had exploded in the breech. However, a hit on one wing was discovered but the Hudson seemed to be unaffected.

With his Hudson virtually unscathed, Terry had time to reflect on the satisfactory sortie. Another Heinkel downed.

By the end of September, the crisis which had held the whole united country in its grip ever since April, was over. It became obvious that the invasion was postponed until at least the following spring. The pilots who had been fighting without relief for the best

---

* The Hudson had fixed front guns in the wings and a twin gun rotatable rear turret operated by an air gunner.

part of six months, could be given long overdue leave. Terry was one of them.

By the time that he returned from leave, despite the fact that the London blitz was now beginning, 206 Squadron was almost back to the balmy days of the 'phoney' war. The bombing raids on enemy ships and ports: the destruction of Hitler's invasion barges; the attacks on his coastal airfields, these dangerous missions were no longer required.

The Hudson had acquitted itself most admirably. It had never been the intention to use it as a strike aircraft but it had out-performed the Blenheims and Battles which had been designed for this role. It had also proved itself to be remarkably endurable. It absorbed hits without damage. It also proved to have almost fighter-class manoeuverability in scraps with the enemy planes. During its brief spell on Atlantic convoy duty, its range had enabled it to reach considerable distances from friendly shores. The order 'off the cuff' had been made during the period when, to build up the RAF, almost *any* order would have been given, and had proved to be an inspired one. It also gave the RAF a healthy regard for American-built planes: which was fortunate as France had several types on order and Britain sensibly had agreed to take on the lot after her ally had been knocked out of the war.

The squadron was back to gunnery exercises: shipping patrols over the North Sea and generally more docile operations. It was during this month that Terry was awarded the Distinguished Flying Cross (DFC) – one of the first pilots in the squadron to receive this distinction.

Terry Bulloch was also due for an operational rest. This was standard practice. A pilot risked his neck against the enemy for so long and would then be taken off ops to recharge his batteries in the comparative calm of an Operational Training Unit (OTU). Here the knowledge he had gained in battle would be imparted to others about to enter the fray for the first time. It was a rest that many pilots desperately needed and which most pilots looked forward to. Some would be counting the days and ticking them off. Their energies would be focussed on when it would be their turn.

Terry, however, had other ideas. He had a horror of Administration work and could be blisteringly critical of those who sat behind desks and sent others to do battle. He felt no need to spend months at an OTU where flying would be dull and limited. He heard that pilots were wanted for a very special and demanding job. It was supposed to be rather hush-hush, and they were asking for volunteers.

Fortunately, the ticks against his name had been piling up. He was recognised as an exceptional pilot; one who had never damaged a plane. He had acquired the reputation of an above-average navigator: one who took this art seriously. He had proved himself master of the Hudson under the most testing of circumstances. He tackled all tasks given him with coolness and courage.* He was on his way to becoming an 'Ace'. The new job would mean giving up his rest period. He would be stepping into the unknown on a risky job, especially at this time of year. Terry simply nodded when this was explained to him. He was a man of few words. The career of this pilot extraordinary was about to take an entirely new twist.

---

* He was so determined to get even with the enemy that he once swept low in his Hudson over Holland and shot a Hun whom he had sighted cycling down an empty street in Ijmuiden.

CHAPTER SEVEN

Atlantic Ferry Pilot

If Terry Bulloch had never seen a Heinkel or a U-boat, the work that he was about to do would have made him an invaluable pilot in the RAF. He had been promoted to the rank of flight lieutenant and had been selected to take part in a vital experiment; to bring American-built planes to Britain by flying them across. The thought of becoming a pioneer Trans-Atlantic Ferry pilot would not have been everyman's idea of a much needed operational rest. In Terry's case, the choice was a wise one. He had established himself as an above average pilot. He had mastered the complexities of a modern American aircraft and he had proved himself to be a keen and conscientious navigator. His superiors thought he was up to the task. So, why not?

More passengers today fly the Atlantic than any other major route. In the winter of 1940 however, it had been flown by very few planes and had just been flown during the winter months *for the first time ever*.

Flight Lieutenant Bulloch and a handful of other selected pilots were ordered to report to Coastal Command HQ at Uxbridge for briefing. The plan was a secret one: so much so in fact that at first no one seemed to know of it or why the pilots were there. Gradually the group were assembled and identified. After that events proceeded apace. The pilots were told to catch the night train from Euston to Glasgow and, once there, to take another train to Greenoch. Here, in company with many other Servicemen, they were ferried to the troopship *Leopoldville* at anchor in the Clyde. This was to take them to Canada.

Terry was at first puzzled that so many other RAF personnel were leaving the country but soon learnt that many on board were the key personnel of Coastal Command's No 2 School of GR.* This was moving, lock, stock and barrel to the safety of Canada. There training could take place without the night bombing raids that had become a feature of the nights of that winter in Britain.

The *Leopoldville* sailed just before Christmas 1940. Initially the ship was part of a convoy but it soon used its superior speed to leave the escorts far behind. However it met up with the battleship *Royal Sovereign* in mid-Atlantic which escorted it to Halifax, Nova Scotia. The reason for being given such an unusually large escort was that a German capital ship was known to be at large in the Atlantic and was thought to be nearby. For the final Saturday of their crossing, they were escorted by a lone Hudson; the only aircraft seen throughout. On 28 December the ship arrived at Halifax where the pilots spent the night on board.

Christmas had been spent on board but the tension was such that it had passed almost unnoticed in a ship that was grossly overcrowded and sailing alone in a sea where losses to U-boats had been so heavy. They were still in Halifax on New Year's Eve. The town was officially 'dry' but some of the party managed to obtain liquor permits and, after much queuing at the liquor shops, were able to obtain the necessary ingredients with which to herald in the year of 1941.

True to form, no one in Canada seemed to know who the pilots were or why they had come. Accordingly a pleasant two weeks were spent enjoying the pleasures that Canada offered. In Nova Scotia, the effects of the war were negligible and pilots who had been in combat, especially any who wore the ribbon of the DFC, were openly treated as heroes.

The small group also managed a few nights in cosmopolitan Montreal where even more delights were on offer. Those who believed in living life to the full, could indulge to their heart's content. The only limit was the $8 per day of their meagre allowance. However some of the ladies of the town were prepared to carry their patriotism to generous proportions. With the war more

---

* By co-incidence, the author, then an instructor with No 2 School of GR, had also been earmarked to sail with the ship but, after an 'altercation' with his CO, he was posted to an Operational Training Unit instead. See his *In Full Flight* (A. Spooner, Macdonald, 1964).

than 3,000 miles away, genuine heroes were few and far between. Many French-Canadians did not approve of the war but the girls knew how to treat men in uniforms.

Finally their posting orders caught up with them. They were to proceed to Los Angeles. There, after an interesting train journey of four days, they were met by a wing commander and taken by bus to the small town of Riverside, 70 miles away, where they were accommodated in the Mission Inn. Work was about to commence.

Each day, Terry and the co-pilot who had been assigned him – a capable young New Zealander with a toothbrush moustache, Flying Officer Ian Patterson – were picked up and taken to March Field, a nearby US Army Air Corps base. There they were attached to the 30th Air Bombardment Squadron. This was a top squadron which operated the much publicised four-engined B-17 bomber – the Flying Fortress. This was the jewel in the USA Army Air Corps' crown and, at the time the most advanced bomber in the world.

For Terry and Ian, it was all very pleasant. The sun shone every day, there was not a vestige of rationing and the war seemed a million miles away. USA was not then at war and California, then as now, revelled in an excess of everything.

It soon transpired that Terry and another experienced pilot, Donald Ross, had been selected to bring across to Britain the first two Flying Fortresses to leave America. But first they had to be taught by the American Army pilots how to manage the big planes. The model awaiting Terry was a B-17C. It was currently still being built by Boeings, but March Field had others very similar.

During this March Field period, the position of Terry, Ian, Ross and the other co-pilot was curious. The USA* was officially a neutral in a European conflict raging 6,000 miles away. The USA Army Air Corps could not be seen openly to be training RAF pilots. To make this matter easier for their American hosts, Terry and the other RAF Brits had been given passports declaring that they were Civil Test Pilots. Their instructions were that when asked what they were doing they were to say that they belonged to the British Purchasing Unit and that they had been sent to USA in connection with a deal to buy aircraft.

This last was all too true. President Roosevelt, highly as he

---

* Pearl Harbour and the US entry into the war came later that year.

personally regarded Britain, was not yet in a position to offer free warplanes or other aid to Britain. The famous 'Lease Lend' Act was not to be signed until March 1941. All supplies had to be paid for by Britain's dwindling pile of pre-war gold. Californians in particular were inclined to be isolationists, often Anti-British ones. Their consent was needed. Fortunately commercial considerations count for much in USA and those who were opposed to allowing Britain to have US warplanes were appeased by the knowledge that they were being paid for at high prices.

During the remaining days of January and right into March 1941 Terry and Donald Ross were carefully taught to handle their new huge aircraft. Flights were made to San Francisco to gaze at the famous Golden Gate bridge, to Tucson in Arizona and as far afield as Texas. With America not at war, there was no need to cut short essential training. Bombing practices were included; both off the coast and at the Muroc Range. Terry was even taught how to use the Norden bombsight, regarded as the best in the world and wrapped in much secrecy. The US Army Air Corps was carrying out its task with full thoroughness. They knew what Terry was being asked to do and they saw to it that he would leave them fully capable of handling, and navigating, the Flying Fortress under all circumstances.

Included in the training were flights up to the lower stratosphere. The B-17s, uniquely, could fly as high as 31,000 feet and Terry had to be accustomed to such rarified atmosphere. Prior to departure for America, he had never flown above 20,000 feet; nor had anyone else in Coastal Command. Instrument flying, night flying, formation flying, were all practised. During the later months Terry was flying as the plane's captain in all but name but, obviously, a US Army Air Corps plane had to be officially in the hands of an Army Air Corps pilot. Ian Patterson seldom got his hands on the B-17 but that was the fate of most co-pilots at the times. (The term co-pilot came later. In 1941 their designation was 2nd pilot.)

By mid-March, the Boeing that Terry and Ian had come so far to collect was ready to be picked up from the giant Boeing factory at Seattle. It had been delayed for two months due to having certain RAF modifications carried out. However a curious 'deal' had first to be performed. In the State of Washington there was a sales tax: one that applied to aircraft. In the neighbouring one of Oregon, no such tax existed. It saved money therefore for Britain to buy the aircraft in Oregon. Accordingly, Colonel Walter R. Peck, the CO of the 30th Bombardment Squadron, and a person with whom Terry had struck up a good friendship, collected the plane from Boeings and flew it the few miles to Portland, Oregon. At Portland the plane, AN 534, was then sold to Terry, the 'test pilot' of the British Purchasing Mission.

As soon as this charade had been completed with Terry 'paying' for the plane with his signature (all on less than £1 per day, his official rate of pay), the journey eastwards, with Terry now officially in command, was commenced. The Flying Fortress had been collected on 18 March and the next day Terry flew it to Boise in Idaho. From there he took it to Salt Lake City and on to Kansas. The plane could have been flown the whole way across America in one day, or two at the most, but Terry had to be ultra cautious. He had to play ball with another commercial consideration. The B-17C was insured but the insurance cover did not include either night flying or flying in poor weather! Half the civilized world was at war but in USA commerce still ruled.

One unexpected by-product of these flights was that Terry, Ross and the others found themselves in the news. The American Press had got wind of the presence of the British pilots and seized upon the story. Their well trained noses for news had rightly made them suspicious that 'things were not quite what they seemed to be'. The Flying Fortress itself was always news. It was the pride of America and its supposed ability to fly into the stratosphere and then, due to the 'Norden bombsight', drop a bomb into a barrel had been blazed across the world.

The war in Europe continued inexorably. London was being bombed nightly, Bulgaria and Romania fell, and in April Greece followed suit. The Press was very alert to the possible involvement of the USA. How far would Roosevelt dare to support Britain? Could America continue to keep out of the war? Boeing bombers being flown by Britons were therefore hot-line news. If, as some shrewd observers were speculating, the Fortresses were about to be flown across the Atlantic, they would make the headlines. Only a handful of pilots in peacetime had ever flown across and, in most cases, those who lived to tell the tale had been acclaimed as heroes with ticker-tape receptions in New York.

Donald Ross had been a test-pilot in peacetime but had been enrolled in the RAF: possibly just for this special job. It would not have been surprising if he had become the unofficial spokesman for the pair flying the Boeings. Press accounts of the time show otherwise.

A new side of Terry Bulloch emerged. The pilot who had been too shy to enter a public restaurant during an early RAF leave, emerged as the group's principal spokesman. Moreover his direct blunt manner of speech clearly went down well with the Press. At first the Boeings attracted little attention. Essentially they were similar to many others of the type. Moreover, for the start of their cross-America journey they were accompanied by Peck in a third Boeing. However at Dayton, Ohio, the Boeings of Terry and Donald Ross, after their arrival at Wright Field, were repainted in RAF camouflage. While at Wright Field, they were also fitted with armour plate, an action which upset their compasses and caused Terry and Donald to carry out fresh compass swings. After the camouflage painting and the addition of RAF roundels there could be no mistaking their ultimate destination.

At Boise, where the threat of a snowstorm held them for three days, the questions had begun. As best they could, they held to their story about being Civil Test Pilots and did their best to conceal their names from the Pressmen but the experienced journalists only had to check the hotel register to discover who they were. Terry at least seems to have kept his christian names from the newshawks. Throughout their stay at Boise he is described as T.M. Bulloch (at times spelt Bullo*ck* to his fury) whereas the other skipper is referred to as Donald Ross and Terry's co-pilot as Ian Patterson.

Terry seems to have been an excellent ambassador for Britain and to have answered most of the questions asked.

'We are confident of winning,' he is quoted as saying.

'So, you think England will win?'

'Oh sure [a favourite expression of his], we knew that all along but we want help from your country: all the help we can get. It's a good cause, you know.' It could hardly have been expressed better. For security reasons Terry declined to say where the two Boeings were heading. When asked outright, he had to admit that the two planes would be flying the Atlantic but when asked when, he brushed the questions aside with a half-smile. 'I can't say things like that, you know. I'm sorry, chaps, but *that* I can't tell you. You know how it is ...'

'How about conditions in England?'

'Not much to worry about,' was the cheerful answer.

During some of the earlier interviews, Terry and Colonel Peck were interviewed together and because of this, he was once described as Captain T.M. Bolen of the US Army Air Corps. For one who disliked greatly to have his name incorrectly spelt, this was doubly annoying. Terry was British and proud of it. He would have been just as annoyed as being called English as he was American. To him English and British were quite different things.

Terry's confident statement that 'Sure, we'll win' was widely reported in a number of papers. At Dayton, Ohio, he appears to have escaped without his name being reported, as he had been instructed. Instead they describe him as being 'short, rugged and bull-doggy' and, although probably having found out his name, respected his wishes not to have it disclosed. They simply refer to him as 'Capt Blrff.'

In one interview, when asked about *English* morale, he replied that the *British* were as cheerful as the Americans around him. Like other Ulstermen (including his father who was prepared to fight the British rather than have them unify Ireland under Rule from Dublin), Terry was prepared to give his life for Britain but had no love for the English. How strongly he felt about this can be gauged from his scrapbook of wartime press cuttings . On the fly-leaf of this, in bold writing, is written:

An Irishman's hatred of England is natural, right and sincere. It is against a rule and a government and is not based on any personal end. It is impersonal and may be most unselfish.

It is signed 'The Bull'.

Curious, paradoxical, typically Irish? And where does Terry Bulloch now live? In England, where else!

Apart from being painted in RAF camouflage and having the well-known roundels displayed, described in one paper as: (American spelling) 'Circles of colored rings on the sides of the fuselage,' the two Boeing bombers also underwent other modifications to suit them to war conditions. At Portland, near where they were handed over (Tax Free!), they were fitted with British self-sealing fuel tanks. These were quite unknown to the Americans who described them as 'shell proof gas-tanks'. The planes were also fitted with perspex astro-domes so that celestial shots could be taken for navigation. Along the way they had a great weight of guns and ammunition removed. The normal B-17s delivered to US Bombardment Squadrons bristled with guns and turrets and it was these heavy arms which had given the plane the name of Flying Fortress.

Terry had to be absolutely sure that the aircraft's compasses would be accurate. His impending flight across the Atlantic would depend upon this. Fortunately he had learnt his navigation seriously and knew that each time guns and turrets were removed, the compasses were liable to have gone haywire. He (and Ross) had to recalibrate (swing) them several times: an exercise that took both time and care, but typical of Terry's thoroughness.

Although the flight eastwards had commenced on 15 March, it was not until 8 April that the Boeings left Dayton, Ohio for British territory at Montreal. Here Terry could revert to RAF uniform. Here also the heavy armour plate which had been added en route was removed in a typical wartime counter-order. This required yet another compass swing.

In Montreal, Terry happened upon a former 206 Squadron pilot, Flying Officer Willie Watson, who had been attending a course. As Willie was anxious to get back into the fray, Terry signed him on as 'an extra navigator'.*

AN534 took its last American flight from Montreal to Gander, in Newfoundland. This island was then a British colony. The big airfield which had been constructed there was the jumping-off point for Terry and the hundreds (thousands) who later flew their planes from the New World to the aid of the Old.

The next day was Good Friday, 11 April. The morning dawned fine and the prospects were that they should soon be on their way. The crew regarded it as a good omen that they had been

* Later, Terry, Willie and the author were all early post-war captains with BOAC, pioneering the Trans-Atlantic route in 1946/7.

accommodated in a hut built for CPR personnel and which had been given the name of 'The Eastbound Inn'.

Gander Met Office was under the control of a rare genius. McTaggart Cowen had little enough to base forecasts on and the flights to Britain were liable to take the best part of a day. However, he acquired the reputation of getting it right. To this day, Terry regards him as the Prince of all Met men. By war's end his fame was acknowledged by all and he remained at Gander, passing out accurate forecasts for flights to Europe for many years after the war but, ironically, his face was partially disfigured from frost-bite. This worthy expert assured the crews that all would be well. McTaggart Cowen did give *positive* assurances, unlike most of his trade.

Terry's plan (and by now he had left Ross and the other Boeing several days behind) was to take off towards dusk, fly through the night so as to arrive over Britain in daylight. Let-down aids were few and unsophisticated and it was usual to find the desired landing aerodrome largely by visual means.

The big Boeing was filled completely with petrol. Checks were made. Spares loaded on board and the crew departed for the traditional pre-ops meal of bacon and eggs; taken on this occasion in portions equal to about two weeks' rations at home. They had also persuaded the cooks to cut them an ample supply of sandwiches for eating on the journey.

As they taxied out, Ross in the second Boeing came in from Montreal. That seemed another good omen. It all seemed almost too good to be true. Soon the first Boeing B-17 for the RAF would be on its way. As they made their final turn onto the take-off runway, the aircraft lurched. With great disappointment they realised that a tyre had burst. Sadly the tyre could not be replaced that evening.

The next day, McTaggart Cowen's forecast was far from good: so gloomy in fact that the flight had to be postponed for 24 hours. It was the same story for the following night and with reluctance, Terry was obliged to postpone for another 24 hours. Before doing this, he had tried to get permission to make the flight to Britain in spite of the low cloud hanging over the country and to fly right across England and, when clear, to let down over the North Sea. This would have eliminated the chances of letting down into high ground. Once over the North Sea, he would turn back west and rely upon his considerable local knowledge of East Coast airfields to find an airfield for landing. He knew that coast 'like the palm of his hand'.

It was a bold idea but permission to try it was not granted. The Atlantic had seldom been flown in winter and he was proposing far more than just the trans-ocean flight. It showed, however that he had acquired vast confidence in the Boeing and its ability to fly the 2100 or so miles to Britain and then to have plenty of petrol remaining. This was no ordinary RAF junior officer. The plans were by a man who had thought out an alternative strategy with the required meteorological and navigational skills to carry it out.

April 13 was cold and clear. The forecast was more promising and the decision to go was made. One person who welcomed this was the cook at Eastbound Inn who for days had cut the sandwiches to be eaten en route.

As before the crew were given the traditional pre-flight meal of eggs and bacon (Canadian portions!) and as the evening light was leaving the sky, Boeing AN534, after consuming about a mile of the long runway for a maximum weight take-off, lifted off the ground at about 135 mph and the first big Boeing bomber earmarked for Britain and the war, was on its way. Its weight was $22\frac{1}{2}$ tons and with its four Wright Cyclone engines of 1200 hp each, it climbed readily to an initial height of 15,000 feet.

At that time of day, there were few airport personnel on duty and it is doubtful that any grasped the significance of the take-off. Almost unnoticed, a key-stone had been laid in the Atlantic Bridge which linked America to Europe.

Terry and Ian Patterson had by then come to good terms with their foreign built machine. Terry's knowledge of navigation and meteorology was put to good use. The winds were favourable, especially at the higher altitudes. By taking the Boeing up to 30,000 feet, a high average speed was maintained and the 1832 nautical miles (2110 miles) to their destination in Scotland were covered in 8.40 hours at an average speed of 245 mph. It established a trans-Atlantic record which was to stand for a long while.

The standard route for those early crossings was between Gander (and less often Goose Bay in Labrador) and Prestwick on the

Ayrshire coast: an aerodrome with a good record of moderately clear weather. However, at this time, Prestwick was being rebuilt with huge ultra wide runways in preparation for the floods of aircraft which, eventually, were to make this historic journey. Accordingly, Terry's destination was the aerodrome at Ayr, Heathfield, a few miles to the south of Prestwick. It had only been commissioned seven days previously and was largely a sea of winter mud.

As the flight had been so swift and uneventful, they didn't dally at Heathfield but took off later the same day and delivered the aircraft to Squire's Gate, Blackpool where the aircraft was due to receive further modifications. This was a relatively small airfield, fashioned out of the race-track at the south end of Blackpool's famous esplanade; just where the trams stopped. However, Terry had no trouble landing the Boeing there.

Although Terry was soon parted from Ian Patterson and lost sight of him for some months (in the way that the RAF constantly chopped and changed crew personnel), Patterson later became involved in a bizarre incident. By November 1942, he had become a squadron leader and a flight commander of 500 squadron. The unit operated Hudsons off the North African coast. Their role was to hunt down the elusive U-boats, many of which were in the Mediterranean at the time. In company with two other Hudsons, he took part in an attack of a U-boat (*U-331*) and so severely damaged it that it could not dive. Its Commander decided to surrender and raised the white flag.

Patterson, in his aircraft, had no means of communicating with the enemy below and for some reason his signals back to base were not being received there. He decided to fly back to Maison Blanche, near Algiers, where he landed and, by telephone, advised the Navy of his 'capture'. That done, he hurried back to the scene of the surrender. The stricken U-boat was still on the surface and still had its white flag hoisted. However, it was under attack. Patterson's earlier signals to base, although not received there, had been picked up by the aircraft carrier *Formidable*. Planes were at once launched: three Albacore torpedo bombers with a fighter escort.

Patterson did his best to protect the U-boat by trying to get his Hudson between it and the attacking planes but to no avail. The

(Right) Preparing to take off from Boise with the first group of Fortresses. From left to right: Donald Ross, Ian Patterson, Terry Bulloch. A member of the crew looks over their shoulders.

(Below) With Greer Garson in Hollywood. Terry is on the far left.

The Flying Fortresses on Wright Field.

At Gander, 1941 on the flight to the UK.

Back again! On the *Tetela* in May 1941. Terry is on the far left, and Donald Ross in the rear.

fighters first machine-gunned the stationary U-boat and torpedo-bombers delivered the coup de grâce. The U-boat blew up with such an explosion that a circling Hudson (there was more than one trying to protect the U-boat) was rocked by the blast and the crew had the horrible sight of seeing bits of bodies *above* it.

Ian Patterson was awarded the Distinguished Service Order and disciplinary action was taken against the Fleet Air Arm Albacore and fighter pilots. It would have been many times more valuable to the Allies to have their hands on a U-boat captured intact. Only two others were ever seized and survived in working order.

U-331, as it happened, was a notorious boat. Earlier it had sunk the British battleship HMS *Barham*: not that the avenging Fleet Air Arm pilots knew this at the time.

Soon after Terry's first flight across the Atlantic (which was followed by Ross in the second Boeing only minutes later), he found himself posted to 120 Squadron though as things turned out he was not to join them until August. He had much enjoyed his 'rest' from operational flying. For one thing, he had discovered that he went down well with the Yanks. He was accustomed to speak his mind on most matters, a habit that did not always please the English but it went down O.K. with the Americans. They tended to do likewise.

If Terry thought that he was about to enter the shooting war again, he was soon disillusioned. 120 Squadron was in the throes of being reborn. It had been earmarked to receive a completely new type of American aircraft about which no details were yet known. It was about to operate from a new airfield that was obviously still under construction. Its personnel were still being assembled from various other units of Coastal Command.

The airfield for 120 Squadron was being built in Northern Ireland to the west of Belfast. When built it would have the longest runways in Coastal Command. Runways of any kind were relatively rare. Most of Coastal Command's airfields, pre-war, were simply grass fields; perfectly adequate for the ladylike Anson. The new airfield had the curious name of Nutts Corner. It was being built alongside a main road along which a bus route ran. A bus-stop was at a corner near a farm which had belonged to a family called Nutt. The bus-stop became known as Nutt's Corner. Has any other major airfield been named after a bus stop? It could only happen in Ireland, perhaps?

The aircraft for which these long runways were being built was the American B-24, the plane which later became known in every theatre of war as the Liberator. Its capabilities were largely unknown at the time that 120 Squadron was being formed but its potential, on paper, was enormous. Like the US-built B-17 which it was designed to supplement or replace, it was capable of operating at heights up to 30,000 feet. Like the B-17, it had four radial engines each of 1200 hp but this time made by Pratt & Whitney. Its similarity to the Flying Fortress stopped there. With its twin rudders, its deep stubby fuselage and its (revolutionary) nose-wheel landing gear, it looked like no other plane. It also had a remarkably long thin wing, so thin that some doubted its strength. On paper, it had about twice the range of any land aircraft flying. If this was the case, then it would be of the utmost value to Coastal Command. The RAF only had a small number on order: barely sufficient for one squadron and, since this had been a 'one-off' batch (originally ordered by the French), there was no guarantee that there would be more.

The aircrew posted to form 120 Squadron were largely survivors. Several had come from two Blenheim squadrons, 53 and 55, which had suffered appalling casualties when maximum effort was being flung into the bombing of Hitler's invasion ports. The Blenheim squadrons had also been decimated during the Battle for France when they had tried to stop the German tide flowing across France. Others, like Terry, had come from Hudson (and Anson) squadrons which had also been heavily engaged during the Battle of Britain period. They were hand-picked pilots who had proved their worth and who also possessed that sixth sense that had enabled them to survive.

Most soon found Nutts Corner pure bliss compared with their former hectic operations. The station was not completed and there were no aircraft to fly. Belfast, which largely ignored rationing ('Oh, sure. That's just an English thing. There's plenty of food around these parts.') was near to hand with clubs and bars that stayed open all day and which, when they did close, were usually open at the back door. Licensing hours in Northern Ireland were 9 am – 9 pm but it was *after* 9 pm that some pubs did most business!

Before Terry was to experience Nutts Corner first-hand, another urgent mission cropped up. Apart from Terry and the RAF few who had gone with him to the USA, Trans-Atlantic ferrying of aircraft was also being attempted by a quite different bunch of airmen. When the idea was first mooted, a few senior BOAC (ex Imperial Airways) commercial pilots had been given the tasks. They were followed by a bunch of what can best be described as American mercenaries. They were pilots of various experience who were in it for dollars and 'kicks'. They were, by British standards, absurdly highly paid and soon became a law unto themselves.

As Prestwick was the principal receiving base for aircraft arriving in Britain (the principal types being the few Liberators for the RAF and the first trickle of some heavily overloaded Hudsons), there were always a few 'Yanks' hanging about there awaiting future orders. They spent much of their waiting time in games of poker. The stakes matched their salaries and these were about $500 or more for each plane delivered. The sight of poker pools swimming with unfamiliar American dollars was both fascinating and galling to the RAF pilots who, like Terry were doing much the same job for about £1 per day.

It was clearly essential to get the Americans back across the Atlantic as rapidly as possible. To solve this the famous BOAC Return Ferry Service was created. BOAC which had engulfed all British commercial aviation for, at least, the duration of the war, was assigned a very few of the first Liberators to arrive. These aircraft – and only these aircraft*, could fly the Atlantic in *both* directions, i.e. they could fly back against the prevailing strong western winds that alone made it possible for medium range aircraft (Hudsons) to cross eastwards.

The service was new; likewise the plane. The risks, especially in winter, were high. One result was that a plane carrying several USA mercenary pilots back to the States crashed soon after takeoff, killing all on board. This Liberator had been converted to a kind of crude passenger carrying aircraft and the numbers killed were embarrassingly high. The American pilots responded by going on

* Outside the few Pan-American Clippers which had started a limited passenger service between Newfoundland (Botwood) and Shannon in Southern Ireland.

'strike'. They were *not* going to trust their lives to any Limey pilots. They demanded to be returned by ship or else the deal was off.

By then, the system was gearing up to a big increase of flights by Hudsons, Fortresses and the much wanted Liberators. Terry was hastily recalled to get back to America and replace the gap caused by the American pilots' actions. Also the Lib crash had temporarily suspended the Return Ferry Service. Consequently Terry had again to cross the Atlantic by ship. The *Leopoldville* journey had been far from enjoyable. This crossing of the ocean was far worse. Fate seemed against it even before it had started. Terry was ordered to join the ship *Tetela*, at Cardiff. The *Tetela* was no swift liner.

At Newport, where he spent the night en route to Cardiff, an air-raid almost bombed him out of bed. Next day, at Cardiff, he was again bombed. It was an auspicious commencement. When at last the convoy of which the *Tetela* was a part did get under way in May 1941 it was attacked in the Minches by one of Germany's long-range aircraft, an FW Condor but fortunately the ship was not hit. The irony was that the convoy, to avoid the dangers of U-boats, had been routed by this very northerly route for safety purposes.

Out in the Atlantic the convoy was a painfully slow one and, as was general, it had far too few escorts; and the few it did have were obliged to leave it to cope as best it could when only half way across. There were never enough Naval vessels to maintain an efficient convoy system.

When the escorts left, the convoy scattered on the theory that if it did run into U-boats, it was better that the ships would all not be in the same area. The *Tetela* was an ex-banana boat and had been built for neither speed nor comfort. Its max speed was about 9 knots.

It was an anxious week or more before the coast of Canada hove into sight. The contrast between this nerve-racking cruise and his own recent smooth flight at 30,000 feet at 250 mph was marked. 'Never again by sea', he vowed to himself. It seemed far worse than near-suicide raids on Hitler's invasion ports.

In Montreal, Terry underwent a 'conversion course' to learn to fly the Liberator. He gathered that this was to be his next delivery flight. Although he had never even *seen* a Liberator, the 'course' consisted of one brief flight from St Hubert's Airport (the RCAF base close to Montreal) during which he was allowed to do three daylight circuits and landings. He was then passed out as fit to command! The contrast between this and the two months that he had spent with the 30th Bombardment Squadron in California could hardly have been more striking. The Atlantic Ferry Service had been thrown into a chaotic state by the abrupt withdrawal of the American pilots. Orders were being issued almost off the cuff as various efforts were made to keep the flow of aircraft crossing.

One example of the haste was that Terry's orders were changed. He was told that his next delivery would be a Hudson, and not a Lib. Terry now found himself, at St Huberts, working alongside several of the ex-Imperial Airways, (now BOAC), veteran pilots and, aloft with Captains Lee and Pat Eaves, flights in Hudsons were made to polish up their celestial navigation. Any crossing in a Hudson was always going to be 'tight' on fuel, west wind or no west wind, and it would be essential to keep on track.

Terry returned from one such night navigation exercise to learn that, within a day or so, he had been earmarked to take a Liberator I aircraft to England in company with Captain Jim Percy, then the rising star among BOAC younger pilots. This was a very definite order and within two days, on 21 June, they were on their way to Gander. The Liberator was AN262. It was only the second time that Terry had sat in the type. At Gander, as the 'ace' Met man declared that the weather ahead was acceptable, they simply refuelled and took off for Britain.

It proved to be an uneventful flight although quite a novel way of becoming familiar with a new type of aircraft! As later events were to show, the two pilots, both superb pilot-navigators, hit it off well. Also Terry and the Liberator fast became 'friends' and together were later to write their names in the history of World War II.

Jim and Terry made quite a team and nine days later they were together again this time flying back to Canada eastwards, against the prevailing wind with thirteen VIPs on board, including some new RAF Ferry pilots. The full virtues of the Liberator were made apparent. They accomplished this eastward flight to Gander in twelve hours fighting strong head-winds all the way. By arrival in Gander Terry had only been in a Liberator four times but was probably the only pilot in the RAF to have crossed the Atlantic both ways in the type: certainly the only one to have crossed the Atlantic in two quite different four-engined American aircraft.

Back in Montreal, where he was briefly reunited with Ian Patterson, Terry found himself in demand both on further astro-nav: training and in teaching other new Atlantic Ferry pilots to handle the Hudson. July, however, was on the whole a quiet restful month for him but not so August. This began with orders to take a Hudson to Britain. This was fine but, he learnt, not with Ian Patterson: not so fine!

On August 1, Terry commenced the journey in the usual way by the flight to Gander. It took 5.35 hours. The aircraft was AE645 and his crew consisted of two American civilians, neither of whom knew anything about navigation. One was a wireless operator and the other a pilot. As the weather forecast was satisfactory, Terry, again, promptly refuelled and, with full tanks, set forth for Britain.

Unlike the big four-engined Fortress and Liberator, the Hudson had but two engines and barely sufficient fuel for the crossing. Terry had to be alert every second of the way. Accurate navigation was essential; also accurate course-keeping. He helped to keep the aircraft on track by taking astro-shots through an open hatch in spite of the appalling cold of this particular action.

Nearing Britain, the weather reports ahead were not too good and, with fuel running low, he decided to land at the new Coastal Command airfield, Limavady, rather awkwardly located between two hills a few miles from Londonderry. It was one that he had not before used and he had been on continuous duty for the best part of 24 hours. However he landed safely.

It is no part of the Terry Bulloch story but it so happens that a young pilot officer of 221 Coastal Command Squadron was in Ops Room when Terry reported his arrival. Although this young Wellington skipper had been in the Command for well over a year, he had no idea that planes were being ferried across the Atlantic and was even more amazed to learn that the medium ranged Lockheed Hudson was being flown across. The young flight lieutenant who had brought it across seemed to take it all as a matter of course: and with impressive calm. The 221 Squadron pilot had not then heard of the name of Terry Bulloch but over the years the two pilots were to see a lot of each other; peacetime as well as war years. It is only recently that the author has deduced that the ferry-pilot whom he saw in Ops Room that morning was the same Terry Bulloch whose biography he is now writing.

Terry was always fit and ever eager to get back into the war. By next morning he was on his way to his destination, Prestwick. The Americans picked up £500 for being his crew members. Terry's reward was an extra ten shillings and six pence; and then only because his flight had been over ten hours and he could therefore claim subsistence money!

With only a few days' leave, Terry soon found himself with 120 Squadron at Nutts Corner. The unit had, at last, received a few Liberators and was preparing to commence their training. During the months that he had been away, he hadn't really missed anything.

Nutts Corner was still being built. Quite sensibly, the runways had been put down early – and it was good to see runways rather than bare grass. The Mess buildings were so unfinished that at one time the officers lacked *any* kind of latrine. Their instructions were to use an adjacent hedgerow but the Group Captain, clearly a sound conservationist, advised them not to use any one place too often! Washing was largely omitted but, once a week, they were taken in a bus to RAF Aldergrove so that they could have bath.

Very little flying had taken place during Terry's absence and, generally, the pilots who had survived by luck and judgement, while so many of their colleagues had been killed, continued to enjoy the relative freedom from 'English' rationing and the plenty of Bushmills whiskey available in Belfast.

Terry's first flight with 120 Squadron in a Lib, took place on 13 August. The plane was a Liberator Mark I. He went up with his flight commander, Flight Lieutenant Harrison, always known as 'Harry John'. The plane was AM911. For the next few days, Terry himself acted as an instructor and passed on the knowledge which he had gained from his Atlantic flights. The squadron was working itself up for the job which it would shortly have to do: to fly deep into the Atlantic and look for U-boats. Terry had also been assigned a crew and began to 'lick them into a good shape'.

Just as Terry was about to be among the first in the new squadron to commence operations, he received an urgent telegram ordering him to report at once to the new airfield at Ayr. He was flown across to Scotland on 24th August and, almost at once put on board a BOAC Liberator which, under a Captain Page, flew the 3,000 and more miles non-stop to Montreal. It had all happened within hours.

Another Hudson needed to be delivered and Terry was to deliver it. He left Montreal in Hudson AE523 a few days later and took the now familiar route, via Gander, back to the UK. As before, his crew consisted of two Americans who could not navigate and virtually the entire flight had to be flown and navigated by himself. This time he landed in UK at his own squadron's airfield of Nutts Corner. Including the flight to Gander, his air-time alone had been in excess of 16 hours. He had had no rest for much longer. After taking the Hudson to Prestwick he was flown back to Nutts Corner. Almost at once he recommenced working his crew up to operational standards. He didn't at all like the idea of others getting ahead of him. It had all taken place so quickly that some of his colleagues did not realise that he had been away.

'I haven't seen you around these last few days, Terry. Where you been?'

'To Montreal and back.'

Terry Bulloch was always a man of few words.

That ended his brief 'rest' period as a Trans-Atlantic ferry pilot. It was a just reward for the hard work he had put in to master the art of navigation. It heightened his interest in meteorology and it confirmed the good opinion he held about American built aircraft. He was to fly millions and millions of more miles during the next 35 years: all in American built aircraft.

If Flight Lieutenant Bulloch had never seen a U-boat, these pioneering flights would have made him an outstanding contributor to Britain's war effort. He had proved that a young RAF pilot could do the job of ferrying aircraft across the then notoriously dangerous and largely unknown route; and could do it as well as the few hand-picked Imperial Airways/BOAC veterans. He had also demonstrated that he could do it as well, or better, than the overpaid American mercenary pilots.

The trickle that Ross, Terry and the few others had started gradually swelled to a flood even to the point, a year or so later, when squadrons of fighter aircraft, flying in formations of up to 30 or more, flew their way to Britain. But by then there were airfields along the way in Greenland, Iceland and the Hebrides; also radio aids to guide the planes and a well organized weather service in and around the ocean itself.

Another tick had been put against the name of Terence Malcolm Bulloch. The Command now knew for certain that they had a pilot of unusually high skill. The next test would be to find out if he could use those skills where they were most urgently wanted. Among the elite of 120 Squadron, would he be able to find and attack U-boats? The Command was doing all it could to help the harassed sailors below but unfortunately, largely to no obvious avail.* Much faith and hope were being placed upon the new aircraft and the new squadron. Were such expectations justified? Time alone would tell.

* Not until 1941 did Coastal Command sink its first U-boat.

CHAPTER EIGHT

120 Squadron

The war had been in progress for two years by the time that Flight Lieutenant T.M. Bulloch, DFC, was posted to fly B-24s on anti-submarine operations for 120 Squadron at Nutts Corner. Two years previously: Terry Bulloch had been an insignificant junior officer; 120 Squadron had been dormant since having been disbanded after World War I; the Consolidated Vultee B-24 bomber was untried; Coastal Command had carried out no anti-U-boat practices and Nutts Corner was a bus-stop.

In retrospect, the decision to assign the majority of the first (French) batch of B-24 bombers, Liberators, to Coastal Command, was one of the key decisions of the war. A few went to BOAC and transport duties for VIPs. The decision was a close one. Not unnaturally Bomber Command laid claims upon this advanced American bomber which could fly faster and higher and for longer distances than any in that Command. Fortunately, Churchill, ever conscious of the need to keep our sea-lanes open, intervened and he was backed by Admiral Sir Dudley Pound.

By 1941, sinkings by U-boats had reached alarming proportions. The only grain of comfort was that sinkings of ships in convoys were considerably less than sinkings elsewhere. Moreover, it was discovered that sinkings of ships in those convoys which had the additional protection of air-cover were considerably less than in those convoys which did not have air-cover.

At first the Navy tried to provide its own air-cover by using their very limited supply of aircraft carriers but after the *Courageous* and then *Glorious* were sunk, this was abandoned. The *Ark Royal* also only narrowly escaped being sunk or seriously damaged by a German torpedo.

Coastal Command was then called on to supply the required

122

air-cover: a difficult task to fulfil since it had neither the planes for the job nor the weapons to sink a U-boat nor had their pilots been trained for the skilled task nor were the Command's few airfields in the correct places: especially after the fall of France and Doenitz's swift establishment of his French Atlantic bases.

Churchill, in a letter to President Roosevelt that helped to get Britain further supplies of Liberators had written: 'It is in shipping and in the power to transport across the oceans that in 1941 the crunch of the war will be felt'. He had also stressed to the War Cabinet that: 'priority be given to fitting Coastal Command planes with ASV (radar)' adding that Coastal Command should have priority in delivery of the new long range Liberator bombers from America. As usual he was right.

The Battle of the Atlantic was always at the forefront of his mind, together with the need to equip Coastal Command with the weapons to combat the U-boat menace.

The Libs which arrived from America had to be much modified: a high-flying bomber and a low-level Coastal plane are very different warplanes. The addition of ASV alone was a major 'mod'. The early sets required the plane to be festooned with additional aerials: along the plane's spine, under its wings and on its sides. The ASV scanner itself was fitted to 'look' forward in an unsightly bulge under the nose. In Ireland, where such a strange protuberance attracted comment, one story which the more gullible Irish swallowed was that the plane's builders had forgotten to allow a space for the pilot's feet and the bulge was to accommodate these!

All this took time, which was why 120 Squadron was left with little to do during the period when Terry was delivering the Fortress, the Lib and the Hudsons from USA. By the time that Terry was able to join the squadron, some of the earlier postings had become quite familiar with such establishments as The Grand Central Hotel, Belfast and a night spot called the 'Four Hundred' where, it was said, the lighting was so dim that, as young Peter Cundy describes it: 'You only recognised your female partner by feel (literally).'

Peter Cundy was one of the few who had survived from the frightful slaughter of 53 and 59 Squadrons – the Blenheim units that had been wiped out in France and again during the invasion scare period of 1940. Like two others, Walton and Wightman, who had survived and who joined 120 Squadron, he had been an Army officer prior to transferring to the RAF. All three turned out to be outstanding Coastal Command pilots.

In September 1941 a new Commanding Officer arrived. This was Wing Commander V.H.A. McBratney, an Irishman. He quickly took in the situation, did not like what he saw and in no time set about licking the new squadron into shape. One early victim of the return of more normal standards of discipline was Peter Cundy who had his leave suspended because of his absence from base one afternoon. Peter was incensed because all he had been doing was playing squash with the Station Commander! He was so fed up that, when next in Belfast he bought one of those horrible 'doggie do' things and left it on McBratney's desk. The point being that McB had a spaniel which spent much time in his office. He adds that, 'Whether or not it was the embarassed look on the spaniel's face or some other matter which pricked McBratney's conscience I shall never know but shortly afterwards I was told that my leave was on again.'

Although he had been absent, on and off, for months, Terry Bulloch found that he was one of the few in his new squadron who had flown or knew anything about the B-24s which they so anxiously awaited. His time in the aircraft was relatively slight but he had flown it both ways across the Atlantic! In reality he had *learnt* to fly it while doing so.

At that time the DFC was a relatively rare decoration in Coastal and the ribbon on Terry's tunic also made him stand out among his fellow pilots. Added to which he was a bit of a loner and did not belong to any of the small cliques which had developed: one from the Blenheim survivors; another from the Auxiliary Air Force Squadrons (500 and 504) which had also supplied several hand-picked pilots. However Terry was no kill-joy and did occasionally accompany Peter and his friends to the Belfast night-spots, accompanied, as Peter Cundy recalls it by a lady 'in a black dress' about whom he refused to be drawn.

When flying began in earnest and the supply of Liberators increased, Terry was among the first to fly them. The two flight commanders were Flight Lieutenant Harrison, 'Harry John', and Dicky Gates.

Ten days after Terry had delivered his Hudson to UK, he and Harry John, in Lib AM911, commenced the squadron's World War II history in B-24s. For the next few days, Terry was busy giving instruction to his fellow pilots: those who would be given commands of aircraft. None before had flown four-engined aircraft or aircraft with a nose, as opposed to a tail-wheel. Not that this was a handicap; quite the reverse in fact.

During that September, Terry began anti-submarine sweeps over the Atlantic. Soon to be followed by the others. His crew included Pilot Officer Dear, second pilot and Sergeant McColl*, a young Scot whom he had found in the hangar and who had responded to the cry for volunteers for a new aircrew category of Flight Engineer. The navigator was Pilot Officer Mitchell and there were three 'Jack of all Trades – their official rank being wireless-operator/air gunners (WOP/AGs for short) but who, in ASV equipped aircraft, had to become ASV watchmen as well. It sounds a lot but over the Atlantic there was little need of air-gunners, although the aircraft was fitted with both tail and forward-firing guns. Again Terry was fortunate in that one of these proved to be outstanding. Sergeant (virtually all WOP/AGs were given this rank) 'Ginger' Turner was one of the few of his trade who seemed to grasp how to get the best out of the ASV aboard.

A major difficulty with these early forms of radar (ASV) was that the device was regarded with such secrecy that the absolute minimum of training was given to the non-commissioned aircrew who were detailed to operate them. As also, it was 'next to impossible' to gain much intelligence from these sets when flying over the heavy seas of the North Atlantic, due to the clutter that filled the tiny viewing screen given back by echoes from the large waves and heaving rollers, it is no wonder that they contributed little to the locating of U-boats. Ginger Turner, however, soon became expert at distinguishing between the more solid return 'blips' from ships etc and the constant flickering returns from the seas below.

A peculiar difficulty with this crew was that although they all spoke the same English language, they did so with very differing

---

* With his uncanny ability to find himself a 'winner' and to retain him against normal policy, this young lad from the hangar, Jock McColl, was to become a key man in Terry's crews not only in 120 Squadron but for years afterwards.

accents. Ginger Turner's vowels were as flat as any Yorkshireman's could be and Jock McColl had a Scottish brogue which could be cut with the proverbial knife. Yet, in the air, their only link with one another was by the headphones which they constantly wore; against which they also had to compete with the constant roar of the plane's four engines.

When Terry was not flying – and, by one means or another, he managed to fly more often than any other pilot in the squadron – he spent many hours in the squadron's Intelligence Office and Ops Room. This way he acquired a close knowledge of where the enemy were most likely to be found, what types of U-boats there were, how they were armed, what their tactics were and even the names of their most publicised 'Aces'. He also gained information about our convoys and their escorts.

Using his own interpretation of how the Battle of the Atlantic was faring and where the next threat to our convoys was most likely to be, he was able to deduce where, and when, U-boats were most threatening. He would then 'arrange' to take the flight to that area. There is no doubt that by these 'arrangements' he upset some of the more junior aircraft captains who were just as keen as he to get to grips with the enemy but not so willing to give up their spare time to studying their tactics.

Terry had seniority on his side plus a reputation: and a fairly hostile approach when riled or thwarted. He was regarded as a figure of some awe by others who had not been awarded the DFC, who were relatively 'green' in general experience and who had not mastered the Atlantic by delivery flights. When Terry 'suggested' in his usual terse manner that, 'I'll take your flight to-morrow and you can have one of mine some other day', there were few junior aircraft commanders prepared to argue the point: and if 'some other day' took a long time to come around, so what? 'There'll be some other time, old chap …'

It did not take long for Terry's tactics and determination to pay off. On his fourth big sweep deep into the Atlantic, he caught sight of his first U-boat. The date was 22 October 1941.

All in all, this was quite a trip for him. He had been sent to find, and protect, convoy SC 89. He arrived to discover that the convoy was being shadowed by a German plane, one of their big

Focke-Wulf 200, Condors. These splendid aircraft (about the only plane which matched the B-24 at the time) would carry out wide sweeps of the Atlantic flying a vast semi-circle from a base in Northern Norway down to one in the Brest area, (or vice versa). If they located a convoy, they would report it and, upon leaving, bomb it as well. They were remarkably efficient, and it is one of the mysteries of the Battle of the Atlantic that greater use was not made of this type of aircraft. Like the Hudson, the Condor was a wartime conversion of a civil aircraft. Like the Hudson, it proved to be a success as a warplane. In some of the months of the war, thanks largely to this lone squadron, German planes sank more tonnage than did the U-boats* although bombing was only their secondary role. Yet by war's end a bare 200 of these had been produced† and most were assigned to transport work or became the personal plane of Germany's War Lords.

The Condor's main Atlantic role was to find, shadow and report the convoys. This was invaluable information for Doenitz. Neither the Lib nor the Condor, both massive four-engined planes, were ever intended for 'dog-fighting' but this did not deter Terry who at once manoeuvered for a stern attack, as per his Hudson days. The Lib Is, as originally delivered to 120 Squadron, had been fitted with four 20mm cannons fixed to fire forward in the aircraft's nose. The thinking was that they might damage U-boats by gunfire. It had not then been appreciated that the U-boats were much too strongly constructed to be seriously harmed by such 'peanuts'.

Although Terry got in a burst of fire, no visible effects could be seen. As is usual over the Atlantic, the area was covered by low cloud and as these unwieldy giants attempted to joust with one another, one or other plane kept disappearing into the 'murk'. In all Terry and a Condor met up about three or four times during the ensuing hours. In all probability it was always the same Condor each time as their numbers were so few that it was unlikely that two would have been in the same vicinity. Several of Terry's bursts of fire – with the rear gunner also occasionally getting in some shots with smaller .303 ammunition, appeared to strike home but nothing dramatic seemed

---

* In April 1941, German aircraft sank 323,000 tons. The U-boat total was 249,000 tons.

† Several *thousands* of Faithful Annie Ansons were built!

to occur within the enemy plane.

Terry's Lib, AM926, appeared to be unscathed but, hours later on the ground, he discovered that one engine had been hit and that a shot from the Condor had passed clean through one propeller blade. However the faithful Pratt and Whitney engines kept turning as if nothing had happened. His most dangerous moments were when the air battle came so close to the sea that both planes, with their big wing-spans, were in danger of hitting a wing tip as they turned and twisted so low down. The most disturbing aspect of this unusual dog-fight was that during the struggle, when the planes were close, Terry and his crew were able to observe that the Condor, like themselves, had been equipped with some 'Christmas tree' looking additional aerials. Were the Germans matching Coastal Command with radar (ASV)? If so, then *both* sides were sharing a common Top Secret!* This would help to explain how it was that these Condors were proving so adept at locating the Allies' convoys. (Not until the Spring of 1943 was it appreciated that Doenitz' Intelligence Unit was reading our signals as well.)

An hour after the jousting had commenced, a U-boat was sighted with its conning-tower awash three miles away on the port bow. Terry had spotted it first. He had such sharp sight that he usually was the first on board to detect an enemy below, although his flying duties restricted his watchkeeping activities. He dived his Lib steeply from 1500 feet and dropped three depth-charges across the track of the fast disappearing U-boat, which was diving frantically. The third depth-charge was estimated as a hit. Its underwater explosion caused a considerable disturbance to the surface about 50-70 feet in diameter. This occurred at the end of the U-boat's track. As usual that was all that the crew, circling above, could see. Sunk? Damaged? Missed? It was impossible to tell which. All that Terry could claim was that it looked 'bang on'. He had dropped three depth-charges but had observed four underwater explosions. Who knew what it meant?

A further hour later, he again resumed the inconclusive air-battle with the same, or another, FW Condor, with no obvious damage to either plane. It was quite an eventful day for the crew and the legend

* This was the case. It was German radar which had picked up the Wellingtons early during the 1939 raids on the Kiel Canal.

Liberator I of 120 Squadron, Nutts Corner.

With the Lib I. From left to right: back row: Jock McColl, Hollies, Ginger Turner, Miller.
Front row: P/O Mitchell, Terry Bulloch, P/O Dear.

Liberator I of 120 Squadron.

Sketch of attack with U-Boat Assessment Form, 25th April 1942.

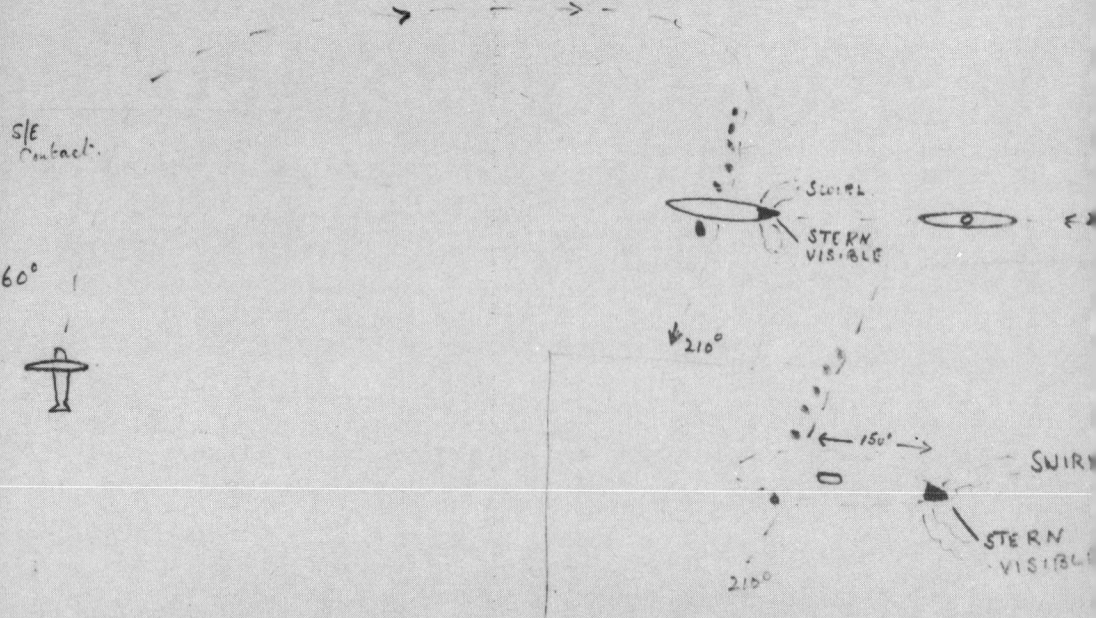

U-BOAT ATTACK ASSESSMENT FORM   Serial No 16

(a)   Date 25th April, 1942   (b) Time of attack 1032

(c)   Aircraft letter and Squadron and Captain of a/c P/120 S/L Bulloch.

(d)   Relevant C.C. Form AUB Serial No. 1

(e)   Details of Report (extracts from Form AUB quoted above) On A/S patrol,
       flying at 1500ft on track 360° in 7/10 cloud base 1500ft. sea rough wind E.
       Vis. 4 miles hazy got an S/E* contact 7' to starb. A/C homed and broke cloud
       on track 210° when contact was estimated 2' away. Immediately sighted a U/B
       on surface right ahead distant 2' in posn. 47° 20'N 20° 20'W Co.270° 6kts.
       A/C attacked from starb quarter releasing from 150' 6 - 250 lb. D.C.s Mk.13
       Pistol set to 25ft depth but spaced to 70 ft while U/B's C.T. and stern were
       still visible. Stick fell in two irregular groups, one on starb bow of U/B and
       other about 150ft ahead of stern. All exploded while stern was still visible
       which was seen going into the last two fountains. 20 secs after, a whitish patch
       of air bubbles about 25 ft across appeared between these last two explosion
       marks. This is confirmed by a photograph.

(f)   Analysis by Naval Staff, based on (d) above. (See C.C.T.M. No.22)

       I consider U/B was straddled by the last two D/C's about half way between
       the bow and C.T. but the large spacing may have resulted in the U/B actually
       being out of lethal range of both D.C.s. The large patch of air bubbles may
       have been the final venting of main ballast as she went under.

       I understand that the irregular and excessive spacing of D.C.'s is due to the
       fact that Liberators have not got the usual British distributors fitted and the
       American Pattern fitted is unsuitable so that each charge has to be released
       by a separate pushing of the button.

(g)   Sketch diagram of attack. [See opposite]

* Secret equipment (i.e. ASV). This is one of the few occasions when ASV *did*
detect a U-boat (thanks to Ginger Turner). *Author.*

of Terry Bulloch with 120 Squadron had begun. All to the good for Terry, too. Who would now dare deny him an extra trip? Terry looks at you when he talks to you and invariably comes straight to the point – 'You won't mind if I take your trip, will you?'

Many strange events take place in wartime: events which in the cool light of post-war days seem to lack all logic. One of these was on 13 December when Terry, in Lib AM 928 was detailed to fly all the way from Ireland to find and to dive bomb a ship near Biarritz, off the French Atlantic coast. The ship was believed to be carrying iron ore from Spain to a French port. The vessel was small, only about 1000 tons, and it is inconceivable that the tonnage of iron ore carried could have affected the mighty war efforts of Nazi Germany.

Soon after dawn Terry found his quarry, as he invariably seemed able to do. It was flying the German flag and was being escorted into Biarritz by a heavily armed Flak-ship of the kind that was normally used to protect U-boats when near to those port areas where attacks from Coastal bombers might be made.*

Terry was no stranger to attacking ships. He had carried out dive-bombing in his Hudson when with 206 Squadron. As seemed usual in Coastal Command at the time, his Lib carried no low-level bombsight. The attack had to be made by eye and the only hope of success was to go in at almost mast height. This had been recognized and were his orders: the bombs had been fitted with an eleven second delay accordingly. Otherwise a hit on the ships so close to the water would have destroyed plane as well as target. In the event, the bombs near-missed but he hit one ship with the cannons.

Both the ore-carrying ship and the flak vessel returned a hail of accurate fire. Terry's Lib suffered damage and the gunner, Sergeant Hollis, was severely wounded in head and face. The port rudder was damaged but fortunately nothing vital was hit to prevent the plane from being able to return. With his gunner badly wounded, Terry set course at once for St Eval, a Coastal Command base in Cornwall. Although this action resulted in Hollis receiving medical assistance as soon as possible, the gunner lost an eye. But the question remains: should one of Coastal Command's few Liberators have been used in this manner for such a trivial target? As it was, Coastal

---

* Attempts were made by light bombers to catch U-boats on the surface as they departed on, or returned from, war cruises.

Command came within inches of losing not only a hard to replace aircraft but the most successful U-boat hunter of all times.

Libs were now arriving in greater numbers. The earlier Lib I had been replaced by a supposed improvement, the Lib II. Against this the squadron was losing aircraft. The type was new and wartime training, as ever, was not to the very maximum as the RAF continued to grow in size. The forty Coastal Squadrons were now largely composed of pilots who, pre-war, had been civilians. One Lib of 120 Squadron was wrecked on landing. Another flew into the Ochil Hills killing all on board. BOAC had lost at least two on their Return Ferry Service.

On one of his few days off, Terry paid his first visit to Buckingham Palace to receive from the hands of King George VI the DFC that he had so richly earned with 206 Squadron. For a second time, Terry was ordered, on 19 December, to take his Lib I (he would have little to do with the supposedly improved Lib IIs) down to the Bay of Biscay. This time the target he had to search for was a more worthwhile one. The heavy German cruiser, *Prinz Eugen* was in Brest with *Scharnhorst* and *Gneisenau* and the Admiralty were ever vigilant, in case they should break out into the Atlantic. By then, Jock McColl, Flight Engineer, and Terry had already found methods of extending the duration of their trips by careful fuel management. The crew hunted for the enemy cruiser for fourteen hours but found nothing. Again, Terry elected to land back at St Eval, since to do so, extended his hours of search. Ginger Turner did report a firm 'blip' on the crude ASV but by the time that Terry could dive, the blip had disappeared. This maddening occurrence was to be repeated many times during the next months. In many cases, there probably *was* a U-boat to be attacked, but the odds were always heavily in favour of the four skilled look-outs on the U-boat being able to pick up the plane long before an attack from the air could be launched.

Three days later, on the 22nd, Terry, while guarding convoy HG 76 far out into the Atlantic, sighted not just one U-boat positioning itself to attack, but three! All spotted him and submerged before he could bring his aircraft into an attacking position. Terry and Jock managed to keep their aircraft in the air for almost sixteen hours but even so, Terry elected to land back at Limavady, near Londonderry as it reduced the return flight by nearly 100 miles and the weather was poor at Nutts Corner and he hadn't fuel in hand to hang about.

120 Squadron was finding U-boats faster than any other in the Command. Its total was already four. All four to the same pilot. His friends now gave him a new name. Although 'The Bull' was still a widely used nickname – and one that suited him so well as it incorporated both his name and his aggressive outlook, many now referred to him as 'Hawkeyes'; equally apt since he alone seemed able to detect the insignificant difference between a half submerged submarine's wake and the 'white-caps' and spume that so frequently blew off the Atlantic waves.

ASV was not finding U-boats as the theorists had hoped. In calmer seas where the waves and rollers would not have given such similar echoing returns, it might have proved invaluable (as indeed did later models in most seas) but that is not to say that ASV I & II were useless or unpopular with the crews. It was probably not liked by the WOP/AGs who now had additional duties aloft and who had to spend so many non-productive hours in the cold cramped positions hastily provided for the ASV 'watcher'. They suffered from eye-strain, headaches and confusion. It was essential to rotate watches every hour or so: otherwise peering into the small hood provided became intolerable. The device did, however, make it many times easier to locate the convoys they had been sent to guard. Dozens of surface ships with large superstructures gave returns which were unmistakable. The device also picked up coastlines and materially helped the planes find their way back to Ireland or the Scottish Isles. Fortunately that scientific genius, Henry (later Sir Henry) Tizard took a keen interest in ASV and did much to ensure that future planes were so designed that the task of continuously monitoring the set, was made easier and less fatiguing for the long suffering WOP/AGs.

U-boats and convoys were not all that Terry Bulloch was finding in the Atlantic. On 2nd January (1942), in AM 925, he located a tanker which had been torpedoed and abandoned. He also found two corvettes nearby and directed them to the stricken ship. Nor did he have to confine his 'Hawkeyes' to the Atlantic. During the same month he was ordered to go on a photo reconnaissance sortie, to seek the mighty German battleship *Tirpitz* thought to be lurking in Trondheim fjord in the north of Norway. In the way that orders were given and countermanded, he was recalled before reaching the area. On another occasion, when ordered to search far north of Scotland, he landed back at Wick: again so that he could extend his search by several hours. Already there were signs that Terry thought things out for himself and landed back where *he* thought was right. The 'loner' was becoming a 'law unto himself'. But no pilot was fighting the war with greater determination or with more thoroughness. McBratney relates. 'He was the supreme Liberator captain. A first-class navigator, an inspiring crew captain and one who knew the value of meteorology and who had made a point of mastering this science as well. As a pilot he was, of course, 'exceptional.'

As 120 Squadron and the enormous range of the Liberators became better known, the squadron was wanted in a dozen places at once: one reason why Churchill never let up in correspondence with Roosevelt about Britain's need for a continuous supply.* Libs from 120 were flying patrols off the coast of Portugal, up into the Arctic, off Norway, around the shores of Iceland and down to the Azores. Occasionally, McBratney had to detach a plane or two for temporary basing at Gibraltar or Cairo, as special assignments appeared. It all had to be done by just one squadron. Others were being mooted, or even forming, but lack of aircraft meant that for a whole year, 120 was the only Liberator unit† in the RAF. The second to be formed was 86 Squadron (Coastal Command).

January and February 1942 were very wet months with little good flying weather. March was also wet and Terry, when taking a Lib to Prestwick (mods were usually done there and were forever being added) skidded off the wet grass into a shallow trench which had been dug in connection with the ever-extending of that important receiving base for Trans-Atlantic flights. The undercarriage collapsed. Terry was not pleased at this blemish on his excellent flying record. He was even more displeased when the report of the accident partially threw the blame on him and not on the chaotic state of the airfield at the time.

* The principal reason the Americans were reluctant to send Britain Liberators 'by the score' was that they were needed for their own Pacific War.

† In theory a squadron might have up to 24 aircraft. In practice the number serviceable was nearer 12.

This brush with officials in the offices of HQ was not to be his last. Being as keen as he was to get to grips with the enemy: to settle the score and to avenge Larmor's death, he had a low opinion of those who sat in offices far from any firing line and issued orders which, on occasion, appeared to be totally divorced from rhyme or reason. Being the outspoken individual that he was, he made no secret of his displeasure. Senior Officers who wore pilots' wings but sat on their fannies and who never came near operational airfields were labelled as 'Windy buggers' and Terry didn't mind who heard him say so. Others were labelled as 'Useless bastards'. Terry held a high opinion of McBratney and didn't mind how tough he was. Although coming from different parts of Ireland, they were both used to speaking their minds and getting on with the business.

It is noticeable that by this time, every trace of shyness seems to have been left behind (or was being well concealed behind a brusque surface manner*) and Terry, as he grew in stature as a wartime 'Ace', had developed the habit of almost barking at complete strangers. He had little time for those who didn't share his enthusiasm for hunting down the enemy. McBratney was also quick to appreciate that Terry did not mind how hard he worked and used him, when not operating his own flights, and other pilots' as well – a habit which McBratney never attempted to stop, as a flight instructor to teach the steady stream of newcomers to the squadron how to fly the B-24.

April saw Terry in action again. This time in Iceland. This island had been forcibly occupied by Britain with American help and unofficial assistance (USA was not in the war at the time). It was a move which most of the inhabitants highly resented, not that they could do anything about it. With Iceland under firm control, it made a lot of sense to send a few Liberators to operate from there. Not for the first time, 120 Squadron had to carve itself into sub-sections. Leaving the bulk of the planes at Nutts Corner, a detachment was sent, to Reyjkavik airfield, scarcely more than a mile

* The author first met Terry late 1943 (or 1944) at a Coastal Command Mess in Northern Ireland. Both were squadron leaders and Liberator captains of different units. The author's attempts to pry from Terry some of the 'secrets' of his renowned successes were met with the reply 'Go and fight your own b— war!' But by next meeting Terry was friendly and pleasant.

from the island's capital of the same name.

It was a sound and obvious choice to put Terry in charge of this detachment. For one thing, those with thoughts about his future were keen to see how this brilliant U-boat hunter responded to having a command of sorts. Operating from Iceland, there were a number of new options open to the squadron. They could sweep the sea-lanes towards Britain, land there and come back next day. From Reykjavik, they could fly even deeper into the Atlantic and, if needs be, terminate the flight in Canada. Above all, they, and they alone in their long-range Liberators, could provide cover for a convoy in the dreaded Gap which existed between the expanse of ocean that could be covered by planes based in Canada or Newfoundland (still a colony) and the expanse that could be covered by planes based in Britain. Admiral Doenitz had become well aware that his U-boats were being inhibited whenever planes could circle around convoys and had been quick to concentrate his attacks in the huge Gap – the Mid-Atlantic Gap, where, so it seemed, no land-based plane could possibly be a threat to his Wolf Packs.

On an early sortie from Iceland on 24 April 1942, Hawkeyes did it again! He gained a measure of surprise and was able to drop a 'stick' of depth-charges, six in all, which appeared to straddle his target. In theory, at least, this should have been the end of the U-boat. However, theory and practice do not always match.

Until the capture intact of *U-570* in August 1941 it had not been fully appreciated how superbly built these comparatively small U-boats were.* Once in British hands, it was soon learnt that they could withstand pressures of up to 14 *tons* per square *inch*. This meant that the 250lb depth-charges being used, had to be dropped with almost incredible accuracy for the welded and riveted hull to be ruptured.

Planes had but one swift opportunity to sink a U-boat. Unlike a ship they could not hang about for hours or days waiting for the enemy to surface while plotting its position beneath the waves by use of hydrophones and/or Asdic. Nor could planes sink U-boats by ramming them or by gunfire. Planes couldn't outsit a U-boat and thus force it to surface for lack of air inside its hull.

---

* The type VIIs were between 700-800 tons.

From planes it all had to be done in one hasty rush during which the depth-charges had to be dropped in exactly the right place. Later a quite clever and easy to use low-level bomb-sight was developed for use by Coastal Command but that came later; likewise the accurate radio altimeter which told the pilot his exact height above the waves: a far superior instrument to the pressure altimeters carried by early Coastal Command planes. To have even considered that he might have sunk a U-boat was a feather in Terry's cap. But most remarkable of all was that he had, in the few months since the squadron had become operational, detected no less than five.

Within ten days, five became six! While defending convoy HG 82, on 3rd May, Hawkeyes sighted and attacked another U-boat, again catching it on the surface in the act of crash-diving. The chances were that the enemy had just managed to win the race against time and get to the safety of the deep. This time eight depth-charges were dropped and, as usual, it was impossible to tell what their effect had been on the retreating enemy. It is noteworthy that in this battle between dedicated killers, both sides were most punctilious about their claims. Post-war records show that U-boat Command's estimates of the tonnage sunk was not grossly exaggerated. It was, not unnaturally, a bit on the high side but not wildly so in a war where propaganda reached unprecedented heights. Coastal Command's record is even more meritorious. Post-war research, shows that it sank *more* U-boats than was claimed! During the war, the Navy were the arbiters of whether a U-boat had been sunk. The tracking room of their Naval Operational Intelligence Centre, under the brilliant RNVR Commander Winn (a peacetime barrister!), had such a shrewd idea of where every U-boat was likely to be, that it could deduce sinkings with remarkable accuracy.

No other U-boat was detected by Terry Bulloch in May: nor in June but during this month he continued to earn his bread in other ways. On 9 June, he located a missing tanker and on the 17th found a lifeboat with 42 survivors in it and guided HMS *Orissa* to the spot. Generally he was far from idle. Some pilots when first promoted to a position of mild authority, tend to hug their new office with some relish. Not so, Terry Bulloch. That month he flew over 100 hours. His annual assessment was due and, to no one's surprise, Terry was officially rated 'Exceptional', both as a pilot and a navigator.

The Lib IIs, which Terry scorned, were better armed and protected than Lib Is but paid for this by having less range. The Lib IIIs tried to make good this important deficiency by finding room for still more petrol tanks. All the time, the maximum weight was being increased but, since the engines were the same, the plane became less manoeuverable and required a longer take-off run. But this was the fate of practically every warplane. If it worked at all, then the rule was to pile on more arms, increase the bomb-load, add more guns or fuel tanks and hope that it would still work!

Terry was, and still is, ultra conservative. If he liked something he stood by it. His Lib I was proving, in his hands and with his eyesight, to be an outstanding success. Why should he change it? In latter post-war years, he adopted the same simple philosophy about the cars he drove. He bought a Vauxhall and liked it, so the next eight or so cars he bought were all the same: mainly Vauxhall VX-90s. Later he discovered Saabs and is now driving about his fourth or fifth Saab 90/900 series.*

It is more than likely that, given the choice, Terry would have stayed with the same second pilot throughout the war: provided always that he met his high standards but, with a rapidly expanding Coastal Command, almost as soon as a second pilot became efficient, he would be whipped away to be given a command of his own: often in a quite different unit. Likewise experienced navigators had to be sent elsewhere; possibly to add 'stuffing' to a crew where a new captain was struggling with his first command.

For these reasons, Second Pilot Dear had been replaced by Pilot Officer Goodfellow and navigator Pilot Officer Mitchell by Pilot Officer Neville. Since Terry almost invariably carried out all the flying tasks and was prepared to take on the navigation as well, these changes did not result in any lack of efficiency of the crew. Terry, however, could not be in *three* places at once and had no option but to leave the duties of the flight engineer and those of the WOP/AGs to others.

* In later years, Terry and the author (both BOAC captains) were sent to Los Angeles to collect a new Douglas airliner for their company. During the days that they spent together Terry ordered the same main meal (Roast beef *au jus*; Baked Idaho; salad on the side) at every restaurant they visited: and usually sent it back if the plate wasn't hot!

It is one of the mysteries in the Command how it was that Terry retained Jock McColl, for the entire war and Ginger Turner for so much of it. When asked outright, he confessed that 'I had a friend, an Irishman, of sorts, in HQ, who was able to wangle things a bit.'

Having by May 1942 attacked more U-boats from the air than any other pilot, Terry had evolved his own firm notion of how the attacks should be made. Earlier he had been scathing about the ineffectiveness of depth-charges even when dropped 'slap' on top of the disappearing swirl left by a diving U-boat. To some degree, this deficiency had been remedied by the switch from TNT to the more powerful Torpex explosive; although a very high degree of accuracy was still required.

Terry's firmly held view about how to attack a U-boat was that, in order to achieve the near-perfect accuracy required (and to counter some of the off-putting variables which would always be unknown) the correct method was to drop the 'stick' of depth-charges more or less *in line* with the track being made by the enemy below. The wind effect and the aircraft's drift might cause them to fall marginally to one side or the other but, he reckoned, this would not matter overmuch. Also, to counter such incalculable minor errors, he aimed to drop the 'stick' not dead in line, but about 30° degrees away from the U-boat's track.

This was almost at right-angles with the officially approved method. This was to drop the depth-charges *across*, rather than in line with, the U-boat's heading.

Having experienced the difficulties at first hand and having thought the matter over with his usual thoroughness, Terry simply went ahead and did what *he* considered was correct. Also, in his usual blunt manner, he made no bones about the subject. There are ways and means of gently persuading your seniors that they have 'got it wrong'. Terry was far too honest a person to attempt any such subtle chicanery. To him the matter was one of vital importance and the sooner everyone woke up to it the better. Coastal Command HQ probably didn't see it in this light!

By war's end, Terry's tactics had become the recognised one. It is, however, unlikely that he endeared himself to the back-room boys who had evolved the original theory. It has truly been said that: 'The one thing for which you are never forgiven is being right'!

By July Terry had been promoted to the rank of squadron leader. That month he flew over 120 hours and used airfields as far apart as Iceland, Cornwall, N. Ireland and several others in England. For once he was operating as most pilots of Coastal Command usually did. He was enduring long hours of fruitless searching: fighting fatigue and cold, being perpetually bumped about as he skirted the low clouds which hung around the Atlantic. The weather was always a factor to be watched, especially for those keen crews which stayed, (or overstayed) for long periods around their convoys in order to provide them with maximum protection. On average, Coastal Command crews flew for over a year before sighting a single U-boat: the majority of anti-U-boat crews never even saw one.

August 1942 was quite another matter. On the 10th, he sighted his seventh U-boat but it was able to submerge before he could get at it. Terry never seems to have panicked. Many a crew, after having searched fruitlessly for a year or more, threw all reason out of the window when at last they did find the elusive enemy. If, as was so often the case, the U-boat dived to safety before the aircraft could get even near to it, they would still drop all their depth-charges 'just in case'. Terry knew too much about his foe to waste D-Cs in this slap-happy manner. He was by nature an impatient man but, when frustrated by a diving sub, he displayed a surprisingly calm cool judgement. Killing U-boats was, to him, a deadly serious matter. He knew from his studies of U-boat tactics, that he had achieved much just by having forced the U-boat to dive. He knew that the convoy, SC 94, would be able to proceed in greater safety.

Two days later he was out over in the Atlantic again searching for the survivors of the SS *Letitia* – a search which, to his annoyance, had to be reduced to a flight of only 11 hours and 40 minutes because of a fuel leak. The thought of turning back never crossed his mind. He flew again to escort another convoy on the 14th and again on 16th in AM917, to give comfort and protection to convoy OS37. This gave him the opportunity to detect his eighth U-boat. For once he was able to catch it on the surface and his 'stick' of six depth-charges, dropped the way that *he* thought they should be dropped, straddled the U-boat with its conning-tower still awash. After the attack, wood wreckage was seen floating on the surface. All he reported was: 'I certainly gave it a severe shaking.'

Deck planking was all too easily dislodged by an attack. Unfortunately it meant little. External fuel tanks could also be ruptured by the exploding depth-charges without mortal damage being inflicted. A shattered oil tank was serious, reduced the U-boat's range and efficiency but no more. To get a kill, it was necessary to rupture that 1 inch solid steel circular hull. That was almost more even than the torpedo depth-charges could do. Post-war records show that Terry's brief comment about his attack of 16th August was indeed a modest one. The U-boat he had attacked was *U-89*, a typical Type VIIC raider. It suffered considerable damage but such was its strength, its deliberately simple design, and the skill of the highly trained Engineer-Officer on board, that it was able to resume patrol later. It would, however, have a chastened crew and one which would view with alarm the prospect of again being surprised from the air when about 1,000 miles from any shore.

For this sortie Terry had taken off from a new airfield, Ballykelly in Northern Ireland and had landed back at another new one in Cornwall some sixteen hours later.

After resting up at Predannack (Cornwall), he set forth again on the 18th to meet convoy SL118. While circling around this, he spotted yet another U-boat. Confirmed in his view by the planks blasted off U-89 about how best to damage them, he again dropped six depth-charges close to the U-boat's track. This time he knew for sure that his aim had been good. The U-boat abandoned all attempts to dive. It had been damaged and was trying frantically to sort itself out. This gave Terry, ignoring the return fire from the U-boat guns, a chance to blast the stationary submarine with his four 20mm cannons. As he swept in, he also dropped the two 'anti-submarine' bombs which he had also put on board, largely as an experiment.* These did not seem to add to the U-boat's plight. After about ten minutes on the surface, while Terry fumed inwardly that he lacked a weapon with which to finish off the enemy, the U-boat gingerly submerged. Again it had been saved by its ability to absorb a close hit and by a dedicated engineer. Oil was leaking from

---

* Terry was always looking for a more lethal weapon than the depth-charges. If given one, he would have sunk about six U-boats already.

it and it was in no fit state to continue with the war. It is now known that this was *U-653* and that it did manage to limp back to port for major repairs that took nearly three months to complete.

Although no U-boat had been sunk SL118 was able to sail on unmolested while back in the French Atlantic ports there would be further worries about attacks taking place from the air in areas where, formerly, U-boats had considered themselves safe from aircraft.

Terry and his crew were delighted. They *knew* that they really had caused serious damage.

The Bull's reputation in the squadron had by then grown to enormous size. It was puzzling, too. How was it that he, and he alone, seemed to find U-boats with such frequency. He had, by then, far exceeded the numbers found by any other whole squadron. He was fast becoming a living legend. His insistence upon operating in the oldest type of Liberator I was also a source of curious comment.

Two days later the Bull again left to give assistance to the same convoy SL118. The sortie was only one of ten hours because he was ordered back to base early where the weather was fast closing in. Only ten hours on patrol was akin to slacking! Accordingly he detailed himself to try again the next day but almost before he could reach SL118, he experienced rare engine trouble and had to return. It was an even shorter trip.

As he had only flown 50 hours that week, he decided to try again the next day, too. This time he managed to complete a more satisfying gruelling 15-plus hours in the air. With honour thus satisfied, he then took two weeks' well-earned leave.

Much of September was taken up instructing 'new boys'. The Liberator IIIs were arriving in numbers and the squadron was being increased in size. Soon, however, he was back in charge of the Iceland detachment and on 1 October he spent all that day sweeping the Northern waters as far north as 60N. As he saw nothing and deemed this a waste of time, he decided to fly again the next day as convoy ONS 134 was in need of support. But again, to no avail.

In Iceland, he was entirely his own 'boss' and could fly as often as he wanted. He largely let the office work look after itself. There always seemed to be a good corporal around who knew how to cope with the 'bumph'. Accordingly, he set out again for the third time on the 4th, this time to guard over HX209, but was recalled for bad weather. Another asset about being in charge of the Iceland detachment was that he was privy to all Intelligence and could see for himself where the convoys were supposed to be and make his own assessment of which ones most needed his help.

By now Terry, for the second time, had been obliged to part with his second pilot. Goodfellow, now a F/O was made a captain of an aircraft and Terry had to break in another newcomer, a Canadian Pilot Officer Thomson. For the same reason, he had had to part with navigator Pilot Officer Neville. This time, however, the replacement was no novice.

The new navigator, Flying Officer Michael Layton had such a good reputation that he had been selected to navigate Churchill on his first visit to Moscow. Whether Terry knew of this ability and managed to wangle the posting to his crew is not known (and Terry is silent on the point).

Layton rapidly convinced Terry that he was not only first-class at his job but also that he could look after the rest of the crew, as required. He soon became the crew's unofficial second commander and relieved his captain of as many routine responsibilities as he could. The crew took to him in a big way. Many a time they had been blasted by one of Terry's quick outbursts and Michael Layton, whom Terry got to trust implicitly, did much to smooth over these temporary situations.

Terry had managed, against all odds, to retain in his crew both Ginger Turner and the faithful Jock McColl. With Layton carrying out the navigation with faultless accuracy, he now had keymen in all three subsidiary key positions. It was an anti-submarine crew par excellence. Perhaps the only drawback about the new arrangements was that there were now two Canadian accents over the inter-comm, to add to Ginger's flat Yorkshire one, Terry's Irish brogue and Jock's bewildering Scotish tones!

Where flying was involved, Terry took his command of the Iceland Flight seriously. When a fellow captain, probably the next most senior and one whom Terry had known for many years, took a short cut over a corner of Iceland and, in Terry's estimation, risked flying into rising ground, Terry promptly sent him back to Nutts

Corner. In operational matters he was only concerned with 100% efficiency and was quick to blast anything less.

Terry had also acquired a dislike for the Military Police. In his eyes they were a bunch of able-bodied men who should have been doing something more useful to help to win the war. His dislike for them was heightened by an incident in Iceland's Borg (best) hotel. The Icelanders never welcomed the 'invasion' of their island and were apt to show their resentment by turning their backs on the activities of the British and American personnel stationed near their capital. Terry, although not a great party man, liked to get 'jugged' up once in a while: often with his crew whom he was apt to blast in the air with no ill-feeling. On one occasion, Terry was part of a rowdy crowd who were making such a noise in this smart hotel, that the manager sent for the Military Police. In due course, an Army SP officer arrived to 'read the riot act'. This was like a 'red rag to the bull'. There were never any half-measures about Terry. If he wanted to get jugged up, then he would do the thing properly. Anything worth doing always had to be done properly with him. In brief, the S.P. officer ended up in the hotel's lake; dumped there by Terry.

No action was taken against Terry but, in HQ where records were kept, it seems likely that at least a question mark would have been placed alongside the growing number of affirmative ticks.

For as long as Squadron Leader Bulloch continued to find and damage U-boats, he could probably have got away with murder.

By 12 October, the ace U-boat hunter was at it again! Sent to guard over convoy ONS136 in almost mid-Atlantic, he soon spotted a U-boat and was able to catch it on the surface. All eight depth-charges were dropped and the aim was good. After the attack, wreckage and oil were seen. More interestingly, during the attack a crew member saw a metal object being blown into the air and later falling with a big splash. As usual, all that Terry claimed was that the U-boat appeared to have been heavily damaged. Later Admiralty were able to confirm that *U-597* had been hit and sunk with the total loss of all aboard.

The score was being truly settled.

This was the first U-boat claimed as destroyed by 120 Squadron. Terry Bulloch had done it again: first in the unit to attack one, first to damage one; first to sink one. His meticulously kept log book merely shows: 'Wreckage and oil seen after attack. Severely damaged. Sighted another U-boat later in 57 29N., 27 49W'. This second one, however could not be attacked. For one thing all depth-charges had been dropped; not that this mattered as it had been able to dive to safety before Terry could reach it.

Four days later, he spied another U-boat. While on escort to convoy SC104 the weather was bad with fog down to the deck. Almost for sure this would have been one picked up by ASV, probably by Ginger Turner who tried to be on watch in front of the set at those times when Terry thought that U-boats would most likely be found. Also, in the calm seas associated with sea fog, ASV would be more effective and less cluttered up by wave returns.

Terry attacked this U-boat but, by his own admission, and according to the high standards he set for himself (as well as others), it was a poor effort. In his Log Book, all he writes is: 'Low visibililty. Unsatisfactory attack. Straddled slightly ahead.' Terry could be as hard on himself as he was with others. When, later, asked how many U-boats he himself spotted and how many were otherwise detected (including by ASV), Terry guessed that he himself had sighted about 70% or perhaps 'only 60-70%.' However Michael Layton, who came to know his captain better than any one else in the war, in answer to the same question asserted:

'Oh, it's always the Bull. Whenever subs are around, his eyes seem to stick out of his head.'

As with his claims, Terry was always both brief and modest in Press interviews. He was quick to hand out praise to his crew. 'They're as keen as mustard. It's all teamwork.' He always also made a point of mentioning that, up front in the plane, he was never in a position to see for himself the immediate result of an attack. 'The rear-gunner gave me a graphic account over the intercomm', was a typical comment.

McColl, always eager to try anything that might help his skipper, made a point of trying to obtain photographic evidence of the after effects of these attacks. One picture of his which shows a piece of metal caught in mid-air at the same level as the low-flying aircraft,

Terry Bulloch's personalised Lib Mk V, BZ 721, showing a shark mortally speared. June 1942.

Depth charge explosions in Terry's attack on *U-653* 18th August 1942 in position 41°46′N 19°40′W, resulting in severe damage.

The attack on 12th October 1942 in which *U-597* was destroyed.

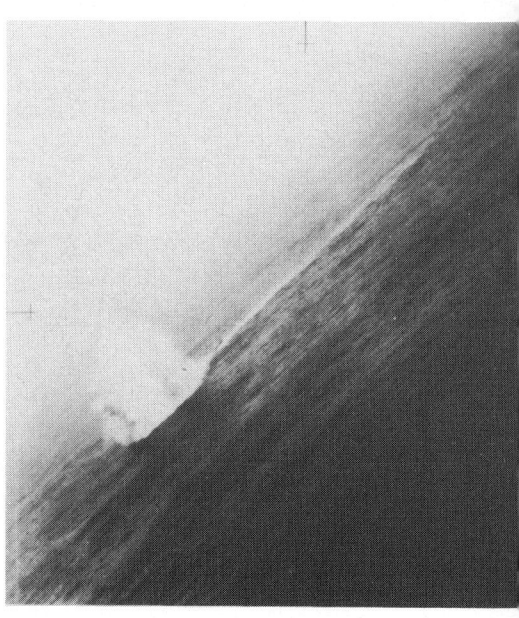

One that got away. An attack on a U-boat while protecting Convoy SC 104. 16th October 1942.

was reproduced in national and weekly papers a dozen times. Britons had little to cheer about and were sickened monthly by the losses at sea as they were announced. The sight of a piece of a U-boat being blown skywards was a welcomed tonic. U-boats were hated and their crews reviled as the 'lowest of the low'. The U-boat crews were actually as tough and brave as those who hunted them. Their officers held that honour – of the German Navy – in high regard. One commander was arrested and executed for cowardice. Their great ace, Otto Kretschmer, when a prisoner of war, arranged a mock court martial of another commander who was thought to have surrendered too easily.

The sinking of *U-597* was not the only success of the CO of the Iceland detachment that October. Before the month was out, while escorting convoy HX212 on 28 October, he broke up a Wolf-Pack of U-boats by diving upon three separate ones. He made no claim to have damaged any and made no attempt to attack the first because he had arrived too long after it had slid under the waves. Likewise the second one. The attack on the third was inconclusive. The main gain to the Allies was, that HX212 sailed on while the U-boats kept out of sight below; fearful of what might happen next. No longer were they the hunters but the hunted.

These attacks and other attacks and sightings by crews of 120 Squadron, which alone could reach into the furthest corners of the Atlantic (as the second Lib Squadron was yet to be formed), deeply perturbed Admiral Doenitz. In his post-war published 'diary' he writes: 'A U-boat reported that, although it was shadowing a convoy 800 miles from the nearest Allied air base, it, and all other U-boats shadowing it were harassed by a four-engined aircraft' Doenitz adds: 'This report came as an unpleasant surprise to the U-boat Command.' Unpleasant or not it was to become an increasingly disturbing factor to Doenitz in his war against the Atlantic convoys in the months to come.

The strange partnership between Terry Bulloch and his beloved Lib I AM929 operating from Reykjavik, was a singularly successful one. Libs were constantly being improved and modified but Terry, who could have had any he liked, remained faithful to his original one. On 5th November, only a week after his scattering of the

U-boats which were lying in wait to slaughter HX212, he was out assisting convoy SC107, well to the south-west of Iceland, in the area 58-59N-32-33W. Sighting a U-boat he swung into an attack. The U-boat was well and truly caught while still on the surface. Using his own, by now well proved method of attack, Terry dropped six depth-charges along the track of the U-boat from stem to stern. Even by his own high standards, he felt obliged to record in his Log Book 'Excellent attack'. The bomb aiming was, as usual, by eye alone.

As expected, the U-boat disappeared in the swirl left by the dive. However when this cleared there were obvious signs of wreckage and oil. A further sign of damage came when later the sea boiled up as if from an eruption below. Yet even this was not conclusive of major damage. A U-boat, after a dive, might be hastily blowing tanks to stabilise itself and to check the crash dive. The compressed air released might burst to the surface in a huge explosion – like bubbles.

Never before had Terry used the words 'Excellent attack', not even when sinking *U-597*. Nor was he proved wrong. Although he was not prepared to claim more than 'Very severe damage; probably destroyed', later analysis confirmed that *U-132* had gone down never to surface again. Another U-boat destroyed with all hands lost. As German records put it: '*U-132 Kapitänleutnant Ernst Vogelsang. Am 5 November 1942 südostlich von Cape Farewell (Grönland) durch feindliche Flugzeuge vernichtet. Totalverlust.*'

If U-boats could be attacked from the air in waters SE of Greenland, then clearly there was no place left for them to hide.

Bearing in mind that, within less than a month, Terry had sent ninety German sailors to a watery grave in circumstances that must have been sheer terror, and mindful of the agony of grief that he had so poignantly had to witness from his brother's widow, he was recently asked if he felt any compassion, then or later, for the loved ones of the enemy; dozens of whom must have had young wives similarly recently married. There was no hesitation in the terse and forthright reply: 'They started this thing, not us.' As usual he wasted no words. As he saw it, it was his job to hunt down U-boats in a war which Hitler had started by his ambitious seizure of vast chunks of

Europe. That was his job and that was what he was doing. 'Fair enough?'

Terry Bulloch sees things in black or white. The Germans were definitely on the black side. To this day he will buy nothing German.

The sinking of *U-132*, was not the end of the day's work. Later he spied another U-boat. How many was it that he had now detected? He had lost count and had to consult his log book to tell. 16, 17 or 18? It was quite a job to tally them up even with his log book. As he had only dropped six depth-charges, he still had a couple left for the new enemy but his one was more alert and managed to escape before Terry could get his unwieldly big-span aircraft into an attacking position. However he was not all that much out of position and deemed it possible at least to frighten the second submarine. All he wrote in his log was: '2 DCs dropped 8 seconds after conning-tower disappeared ...'. But another U-boat would never again feel quite so safe. Another prowler had been thrown off the scent. Another convoy sailed safely on.

Not surprisingly, decorations for Terry were awarded. He earned each several times over.

Coastal Command, for all its forty squadrons, so seldom located and attacked U-boats* that any pilot who had tracked down one or two and who had managed to get in any kind of promising attack (with the usual inconclusive results) could expect to be rewarded with a DFC or DFM. However these awards took time to be approved and officially promulgated through Channels. Possibly this may have been one reason why Terry didn't receive a Bar to the DFC which he had won ship-busting on Hudsons until he had attacked seven U-boats. It was awarded in October 1942. Not until he had officially sunk two did he receive the considerably higher award of the DSO (Distinguished Service Order).

In normal circumstances at that time a confirmed kill was so rare that the successful pilot almost always received a DSO.† In Terry's case he had to sink two. Perhaps again, he was moving too fast for

---

* It was not until the Spring of 1943 that Coastal Command aircraft really began to find U-boats in great numbers. By then they were equipping Squadrons with the power Leigh searchlight and the efficient ASV Mark III.

† The DFM if not commissioned or, later, the CGM.

the system. His DSO came through on 1st December. To an
impartial observer, there seems to have been almost a reluctance to
pin medals on the great U-boat hunter. Could it have been that
Command could scarcely credit that one pilot was finding so many
more U-boats than all the others? Yet his claims were the epitome of
modesty: as unvarnished as they could be. A more likely
explanation of almost reluctance to acknowledge his feats by the
usual awards is that his outspoken criticism of others, often men in
high places, may have come home to roost. Had he trodden on too
many corns? Had one of his so-called 'Windy buggers' or 'Useless
bastards' become aware of his comment? The act of tossing an Army
officer of their Military Police into a swimming pool might have
been taken into account? Also, there really was an almost logistical
problem of how to decorate a pilot who, month after month,
out-performed whole squadrons with personal feats which merited
decorations.

November 1942 was a month of exceptionally foul weather.
Visibility was near zero. Strong winds swept the airfields. The rain
and snow lashed down. Runways were covered in slush: the planes
with ice. Little flying took place. The U-boats made the most of it.
The crews, too, had to struggle daily against the unfriendly elements
but they were the cream of a determined nation. They were well
trained and superbly led. All were volunteers; few were ardent Nazis
or brutally inclined. They fought against cold, fatigue, cramped
quarters, poor food, perpetual artificial light, ghastly odours and
insanitary conditions, denied even washing water. They would be on
patrol for as long as four weeks at a time: occasionally even longer
when refuelled and replenished with torpedoes and rations from the
'Milch Cow' bigger submarines, despatched for this purpose. As
with the Coastal Command crews, virtually all, commanders
included, were under 30 years old.

U-boat numbers were on the German side. Doenitz had managed
to obtain enough steel and man-power to build up his fleet to
something closer to the size he wanted. Hitler only very grudgingly
provided him with the priority of resources he sought. His eyes
were for ever set upon conquest by land although after the winter
campaign in Russia had ground to a halt (for the second winter
running), there was only one way that he could hope to win the war

in Europe: on the sea by his U-boats*. Not that he could see it this way.

Doenitz had started the war with a mere tenth of the U-boat fleet that he had planned in 1937. However by December 1942 his fleet had grown to a massive 382 (he would have liked 1,000 at least). Yet the more ominous fact was that it was still growing at the rate of about 20 new U-boats commissioned *per month*.

It is little wonder that, with the long-range planes almost grounded by the weather, November 1942 was to be the record month for tonnage sunk by U-boats. Nearly three-quarters of a million tons of Allied shipping with scores of priceless cargo were sent to the bottom: far more than the Allies' shipyards could replace. Worse still, the merchant seamen who were lost were irreplaceable. The killings at sea had to be stopped somehow. Otherwise the war in Europe was lost.

Doenitz, too, seems to have realised that the Battle of the Atlantic had reached a stage where one side or the other must dominate. On the one hand, he now had something like the size of fleet he had long wanted. On the other hand Allied aircraft were a growing threat. His U-boats were being detected as never before: at night, too, as it was in darkness that ASV really came into its own. A spectacular success either way could tip the balance. The Battle hung in the balance.

News reached the German Command that two massive convoys were being assembled at Halifax – the one sure ice-free port in Canada at that time of year. He had plenty of U-boats at sea. The weather was inhibiting the new enemy – the long-range aircraft which appeared, against all logic, to harass and attack his U-boats in their 'happy hunting ground' – the notorious Gap. This could be the greatest ever slaughter of Allied ships. Such a success would show Hitler what the U-boats could really achieve if given top priority. Britain could be isolated. American supplies would not reach her and there could be no question of American troops arriving en masse as per 1917-18. The convoys sailed. They were picked up and shadowed almost at once. Doenitz's patrols were in

---

* After the sinking of the *Bismarck* ex-Corporal Hitler, never ever Navy-minded, gave up all attempts to send his big ships – fine as they were, into the Atlantic.

position awaiting them. U-boats were Wolf Packs summoned from far and near. The weather during those first days of December continued to handicap the flyers. Both convoys were heading for the Gap. The omens for the killers were all good.

But in war, the unexpected so often seems to upset the best laid plans. Up in Iceland, Terry Bulloch and the even younger Squadron Leader Isted were cooling their heels but within a week both would be part – a vital part – of the Day to Remember.

CHAPTER NINE

The Bull has his Ups and Downs

After the Day to Remember, Terry Bulloch was made an offer that was probably unique. Although he was not a Regular Officer but one on a pre-war Short Service Commission, he was advised that, if he was prepared to attend a lengthy Admin. course at Cranwell College, the RAF's university, he could return to 120 Squadron as its Commanding Officer, a position which would mean promotion to Wing Commander. It wasn't difficult to appreciate that it would also mean much more than that: almost for sure, that his retention in the RAF after the war and after the termination of his Short Service contract, would be assured. He was being invited to 'cross the vale' which divided the few career-minded Regulars from the tens of thousands of wartime recruits and Short Service intakes.

It can readily be imagined that, before the offer was made, there could have been quite a conflict within the Command. The traditionalists would be against it and could quote Terry's moments of indiscipline: the HMS *Nelson* incident, the Iceland hotel one. Even his reputation as 'a bit of a loner' might have been held against him. On the other hand, there could have been those who regarded 'winning the war' as transcending all such reservations.

In the end, the offer was made. Terry's few brushes with officialdom were forgotten, or at least overlooked. The regulars were prepared to be irregular for once.

Terry Bulloch turned the offer down flat. He never had much time for those who sat in offices and ordered others into action. He knew well that a wing commander of a squadron did far less flying than any other pilot: a Wing Co never even had a regular crew. He decided that, with the outcome of the Battle of the Atlantic poised very much in the balance, the offer was not for him.

Subsequent events point to his decision to refuse to join the 'élite', i.e. the Cranwell trained officers, as being a watershed in his relationship with his seniors in CCHQ. Certainly the offer was never repeated and for the next three years Terry was to remain a squadron leader while others junior to him and with far less impressive records were promoted above him. Terry thought that he was doing what he should be doing. HQ thought that he had bitten the hand stretched out to feed him.

Terry has always been a patently honest man. When asked by the author if he would have wanted to stay in the RAF after the war, he replied that he would have liked to have done so. After all, he had been trying to become a regular officer since almost Prep-school days. 'But they never asked me to stay on. They seemed anxious to get rid of me in spite of which they buggered me up by keeping me busy on transport work with the result that I missed my rightful de-mob date. This meant that I couldn't get into BOAC straight away and lost out on their seniority roll; and was put behind people like you. Blast you!'

Another outcome was that just four days after writing his name, and the name of the Command, into the history books on 8 December – Terry Bulloch was posted from Coastal to Ferry Command with orders to report to Montreal.

First, however, there was a spell of leave to enjoy. This was followed by another investiture for the bar to his DSO and a surprising publicity campaign. Terry faced the Press and gave talks over the radio, much as he had done earlier in USA, with a blunt directness that matched the grim mood of the day. Here was a realist without platitudes or 'bull'. In his talks he gave much credit to others in the crew and it was on his recommendation that Layton, McColl and Turner all received the awards that they had deserved. Terry was no seeker after publicity but he took to the limelight as naturally as he flew aircraft. He simply said what he thought; the only inhibition was that various subjects (ASV for one) were taboo for security reasons.

Although adroit at handling the Press, his parents could not get a word out of him at home. As Yvonne recalls, 'All he would say to Mummy was, "I'll tell you after the war" ' and even this was qualified by 'maybe'. Terry can turn on an impish smile and it is easy to imagine that this was one such occasion.

For a whole month, for the only time during the war, Terry never flew an aircraft. Then on 10th January, he found himself in a VIP aircraft as a passenger, side by side with Prince Bernhard of the Netherlands who was moving to Canada. They flew the Atlantic in Liberator AL512 as far as Montreal then in a Hudson for the final leg to Ottawa, which only had a small airport. Terry was in Canada for a lecture tour on anti-submarine tactics to Canadian camps and bases. The French Canadians were very luke-warm about the war: so much so that in the Province of Quebec (their stronghold) conscription had not been enforced. 'Pep' talks from one who had been in the thick of it could result in volunteers. This was familiar ground to Terry. The same 'anti-English' attitude had divided his Ulster which also had failed to make conscription compulsory. There also the populace were divided into Catholic and Protestant communities. In both cases, French-Canadians and Ulstermen volunteered in large numbers but there was not the same united determination as existed in the rest of Britain and in her other overseas Commonwealth countries. Terry can recall somebody he knew who refused to join up. To this day, some, including Terry, have ostracised him.

In Canada, Terry was joined in his lecturing tours by Michael Layton, 'local boy made good'. The two had become close friends and when in Montreal, Terry stayed with Layton's parents. Life was comfortable. Canadians had far fewer restrictions to bear than back home. The campaign took him in various aircraft (all of which he tried to fly, whether or not he was familiar with them!) to Moncton, Dartmouth, Sydney, Gander, Torbay and up to Goose Bay in Labrador, also still a Colony. He also visited Prince Edward Island flying himself there in 'Faithful Annie' once again.

It wasn't Terry's idea of war but, if a pilot of his fame had to be rested (while they wondered, perhaps, what next to do with him?), it made sense to use him in this way. At much the same time, Group Captain Leonard Cheshire, VC, DSO, DFC of Bomber Command was being used on a similar mission in the USA.

By the end of February 1943, Terry had had more than enough of his role as a propagandist. It was not really his forte; pleasant as the intermission was. He was delighted to be told, therefore, that his request for more action had been granted. He was to deliver a Liberator to the UK and stay there.

FL981 was a Liberator V. The number of versions that were produced of this excellent plane probably ran into a hundred or more by war's end. The US Army wanted various models; so did the US Navy. Bomber Command wanted, and got, some which were extensively used in the Middle and Far East. Transport versions appeared. Coastal Command alone used nearly a dozen different Marks. It had become the plane that everyone wanted. Fortunately the vast Willow Run factory at Detroit was churning out models at an astonishing rate. A Ford production line at its best. By war's end over 20,000 had been produced: more than any other Allied plane; yet it was one of the biggest.

By 1943, Terry thought nothing of delivering planes across the Atlantic. He had great faith in the Liberator and, with a BOAC crew, soon handed it over at Prestwick. He had dispensed with the usual test-flight and, at Gander, merely re-fuelled and carried straight on. He seems to have been eager to get back into the war proper.

Terry Bulloch was back but what to do with him? This was Coastal's problem. His rank and experience merited him being given a position in a squadron as a Flight Commander. This was the stepping stone to taking over a squadron. But he had turned that chance down.

An obvious, if temporary, solution was to post him to the Heavy Conversion Unit which had been formed to train pilots to fly Liberators. The Command now had several squadrons of these and who better to make Chief Instructor of the Unit than the pilot who knew the plane best. It could even have been HQ's way of giving Terry a second chance to see how he responded to a position of authority?

The Heavy Conversion Unit was based at Beaulieu, an airfield hacked out of the New Forest*. Terry made a good and generally patient flight instructor. In the air he acted like a good professional. The office work amounted to very litle and 'a good Corporal always seemed to pop up somewhere'. This left him free to fly almost as much as he wanted; and in his case, this meant virtually every day, often several times a day. Compared to U-boat bashing it seemed a

---

* This is an indication of the control of the air in and around the Channel. Two years earlier, no training would have been attempted so close to occupied France.

little tame. 'All right but not active enough' were his words.

For how long Chief Instructor Bulloch would have remained at Beaulieu but for a certain incident cannot be known. He flew hard during the remainder of April and when not with pupils, was prone to go flying 'just for fun sometimes' in one or other of the small planes which Beaulieu had collected.

Terry also managed to get involved in the testing of some 'Secret Equipment' (to quote from his Log Book). This was ASV Mark III – a vastly improved version of the earlier equipment and, for the first time, a really effective radar device for Coastal Command. It operated in a frequency range that the Germans couldn't even credit as possible, because they had not yet conceived the magnetron value. It required no ugly (and drag producing) outside array of additional aerials. It was many times easier to interpret and presented the information in a readily acceptable form – the Planned Position Indicator.

Terry enjoyed this experimental work. He knew the limitations of the earlier ASV and, as ever, was keen to make U-boat hunting and killing easier and more effective. It was fortunate that he had begun this work and knew some of those who were in charge of it. He was about to be removed abruptly from his position of CFI at Beaulieu.

Terry Bulloch was on a night detail with pupils when a rare alert was sounded. A few Focke-Wulf 190 fighter-bombers were bombing nearby Bournemouth. By 1943, Germany had been reduced to making quick sneak raids on Britain with fighters equipped with a few bombs. It was all that the once proud Luftwaffe dared to do.

The order, quite naturally, went out to all planes in the air to douse all their lights and keep clear of airfields until the raid (which wouldn't last long) was over.

Terry didn't like such an order. It smacked of cowardice: to have to hide away for fear of being attacked. Accordingly he decided that he, at least, would show that there was *one* RAF pilot who didn't give a damn about the Luftwaffe fighters. (The Focke-Wulf 190, Germany's best fighter of the war, should have been able to polish off a Liberator with ease).

Terry did douse his lights but decided to come back and land. The airfield at Beaulieu was, sensibly, 100% blacked out. This gave Terry a problem. He needed light to get down. He had the solution on board. The Lib he was flying was one of those that had been fitted with the 2,000,000 candle power Leigh Light – the searchlight which (with the new ASV) was to cause havoc among the U-boats at night. It was powerful in the extreme. It not only illuminated Beaulieu in full but wide areas of the countryside as well.

Terry had defied orders. His provocative act of defiance was sheer bravado but it had made him feel good. No doubt, months of propagandising in UK and Canada followed by gentle circuits and bumps with the new boys on Libs had built up frustration. Defying the Jerries was 'more like it'.

As he admitted with his characteristic smile 'I had ceased to be the Chief Flying Instructor by the next day!'

The Bull, however, had quite a knack of managing to do what he wanted and with whom. He had become interested in experimental work and (did he still have that Irish friend in postings in HQ?) was at once sent to Boscombe Down, the RAF's main experimental airfield. And who did he take with him as his Flight Engineer? Jock McColl, of course.

At Boscombe Down Terry threw himself immediately into the task of perfecting the new ASV Mark III. The 'enemy' whom he located almost daily was HMS submarine *H32*. It didn't take Terry long to realise that the new ASV was a winner all the way. It had been fitted to other aircraft and the Lib had no difficulty in accommodating yet another addition: and without even a bulge in the nose as a retractable scanner ('dustbin') was designed to be raised or lowered amidships.

At Boscombe Down Terry also contacted Wing Commander Leigh, the inventor of the Leigh Light. Trials were taking place to determine where best also to add this device to the Liberators; and how best it should be used by the Liberator squadrons being provided with it. On several occasions Leigh flew aloft with Terry and they worked closely.

Other trials which were being carried out at Boscombe Down with Liberators were: the fitting of a new forward firing gun turret (Terry relished this) and, something that he had never needed but which was greatly demanded elsewhere – a simple but effective low-level bomb sight.

Always a student of meteorology, Terry had been as frustrated as most pilots by being obliged to turn early for home on account of the weather at base clamping down. The need for a means of being able to land in near zero visibility and with clouds almost on the deck, was great. At Boscombe Down, a device, code-named BABS was being tested. This made excellent use of the improved capabilities of ASV Mark III and enabled a pilot to be 'talked down' safely in almost any weather by one of the WOP/AGs within the aircraft.

By these various improvements, Boscombe Down was supplying the answers to nearly all the vexing questions that Terry had been asking since first he went U-boat hunting with 120 Squadron. His biggest complaint, however, had always been the relative ineffectiveness of the (naval) depth-charges carried on board. If he had been armed with a more deadly weapon, he would have sunk a dozen or more subs; not just three for sure.

Boscombe Down was again coming up with the answers. The Unit with Terry taking part, was in the process of adding two new killers to the Lib's arsenal. One device was a homing torpedo to be dropped immediately after a U-boat had won the race for safety and submerged. This was regarded as Top Secret. A nation which depended upon ships reaching its ports was almost fearful of perfecting a homing torpedo. The Germans had tried one* and, until countered, it had caused alarm and damage.

The torpedo was so secret that the crew had to be absent while it was installed in the aircraft. A lorry would drive up with a huge sheet hiding whatever it carried. Another huge sheet would be rigged between lory and aircraft bomb bay. No passer-by could catch even a glimpse of what was being loaded. To compound the secrecy, the torpedo was given the entirely false name of 'Mark 24 Mine', although it was no such thing.

The 'joke' was that, as this stubby torpedo was housed in the Lib's bomb bay and as the WOP/AGs had to walk along the cat-walk in the bomb bay on every occasion when they changed positions (frequently during each flight) they actually had to squeeze past and brush against a weapon which, officially, they were not supposed to know existed!

---

* It homed onto the noise made by ships' propellers. The counter was to trail a noise-making device ('clapper') about 1000 feet behind the ships.

A snag was that, in order to maintain secrecy, if by chance a plane carrying this device, (variously nicknamed 'Baby': 'Wandering Willie' etc) had to land back with this on board away from base due to weather, the captain was forbidden to leave the plane. The author can still remember having to spend a whole winter's night sitting in a freezing cold plane after having completed a tiring 14-15 hour flight!

Wandering Willie would probably have played a bigger part if the war had continued longer. One difficulty was that, since it was designed to hit and sink a U-boat *after* it had dived (and it was lethal enough to destroy it with a single hit for certain), there could never be absolute certainty that it had done its job. That U-boat would never be seen again.

Terry had mixed views about Wandering Willie (or Wandering Annie as some called it). However he had no doubts about Rocket Projectiles, always referred to as 'RPs'.

In Squadron Leader Bulloch's eyes, RPs were just what he had been wanting ever since first becoming an anti-submarine pilot. The rockets were small and this meant that the Lib could carry a dozen or so on top of all else. They were blazed off at the then almost unheard of velocities: well over 1,000 mph. They relied upon their striking power to destroy. They contained no explosive; just a solid head that would literally go through anything they hit. Not even the tough U-boat hull could withstand such a force. They could be dropped low without risk of damaging the plane: and at any speed.

Terry threw himself into these trials. Much had to be decided. At what height should the dive commence? At what angle should the plane be diving? Would they, as some feared, cause the delivering aircraft to be engulfed in, and damaged by, the great whoosh of flames as they ignited? Others thought that the reaction to the blast-off might cause the aircraft to shudder to a stall or even tear off the wings.

Terry took care of all these matters. An aiming sight was developed and Terry soon was able to demonstrate that if the Lib started its dive at 2,000 feet at an angle of 20 degrees, the RPs not only entered the water at a satisfactory angle but, due to the density of the water, shot along just underneath and then re-emerged, still travelling at the speed of a bullet. As someone remarked: 'Just like a performing school of dolphins speeded up to 1,000 mph.'

It was decided to mount the RPs in the Lib on a pair of short stubby extra 'wings' protruding from the lower fuselage on either side (sponsons). Six could be carried on rails under each sponson and it was so arranged that they dropped free an inch or two before blasting off. This was to save the plane from the vicious backlash. As they fired, with a deafening roar, a long sheet of flame ripped backwards. This, at first, scared the living daylights of the gunners manning the guns in the side (another addition).

Terry was so pleased with the way that the RPs worked and the various operational techniques which he helped to develop, that for the second time in his career he applied the word 'Excellent' to the results of the trials. It was not a word that he normally used.

For the trials he used a wreck off Selsey Bill (another indication of the degree that the RAF now ruled the airspace over the Channel) and was soon blasting great chunks out of it.

An important technique was to pull out of the dive *gently*. The long thin Davis wing of the Liberator was not intended for dive bombing. Terry solved this by easing the plane back to level flight by winding on degrees of trim on the adjustable tail-plane rather than hauling back on the yoke in his hands. This avoided overstressing or even wrecking the heavily laden Liberator V. Using this technique the plane levelled at about 50-100 feet. It was all done in only just over a month, at the end of which Terry declared that the system was 'OK' for operations. In addition, he managed to arrange (or wangle) it so that he and his experimental crew were immediately attached temporarily to 224 Squadron with their rocket equipped Libs. As before, Jock McColl was his flight engineer, now a warrant officer. The crew also contained a senior armament officer and another commissioned WOP/AG, Pilot Officer Sandy Lewis.

Terry was not exactly welcomed by 224 Squadron. Like other squadrons, 224 had a balanced complement: a wing commander as CO; two squadron leaders as the respective flight commanders etc, and also a full quota of aircraft. The unexpected arrival of the legendary Terry Bulloch, with far more decorations on his tunic than seen in Coastal Command before and with his own aircraft with senior gunners and specialists aboard rather upset the neat apple cart. This was the start of the quip.

'We've got Terry Bulloch BOAC* with us.'

'BOAC? Why BOAC?'

'Bulloch's Own Airforce Corporation!'

No 224 Squadron were based at St Eval and, in company with nearly a dozen other squadrons (many with Libs), were engaged in the task of bottling up the U-boats by flying non-stop patrols across the Bay of Biscay, one aircraft being relieved by the next etc. Coastal called it 'the unclimbable fence' and it had driven Doenitz almost to desperation. U-boats crossing the Bay on the surface were almost always detected.

Never one to waste time, Terry put himself on extra patrol within a couple of days of announcing his arrival at St Eval. And again two days later. For this second operation, on 4th July, he had armed his Lib BZ72 with the full quota of twelve RPs, a bomb bay of eight depth-charges and had added at the last minute a 'Wandering Willie' (or 'Wandering Annie') 'Mark 24 Mine' i.e. the secret homing torpedo. His second pilot, also brought from Boscombe Down, was a Sergeant Lord.

The patrol was to the southern end of the Bay of Biscay. U-boats were trying to circumvent the Unclimbable Fence by hugging the French coast southwards and entering the Atlantic near Cape Finisterre. After about five hours, Terry, with his wonderful sight, again sighted a U-boat. He had been alerted of the possibility by a look-out on the port side but this crewman, like all on board except McColl, did not really know what it was that they were looking for. The wake of a U-boat was similar to a patch of rough 'white water' but Terry knew at once: who better?

The drill which Terry had worked out was to fire two RPs from each side in the dive at 800 feet: another salvo of four at 600 feet and the final two pairs at 500 feet, after which he would start to trim the adjustable tail-plane to get the aircraft, oh-so-gently, level again. The big Lib would be within 100 feet or less of the sea at the end of this delicate manoeuvre.

It all went just as he had hoped and all aboard were greatly cheered when Sandy Lewis, who was in the best position to see, reported that he had seen eight of the 'porpoises' flash into the

* Then the one and only national airline British Overseas Airways Corporation.

(Left) One that didn't get away. *U-132* is attacked and disappears for ever as depth charges explode around her. 5th November 1942.

(Below) Bulloch in flying gear with Jock McColl.

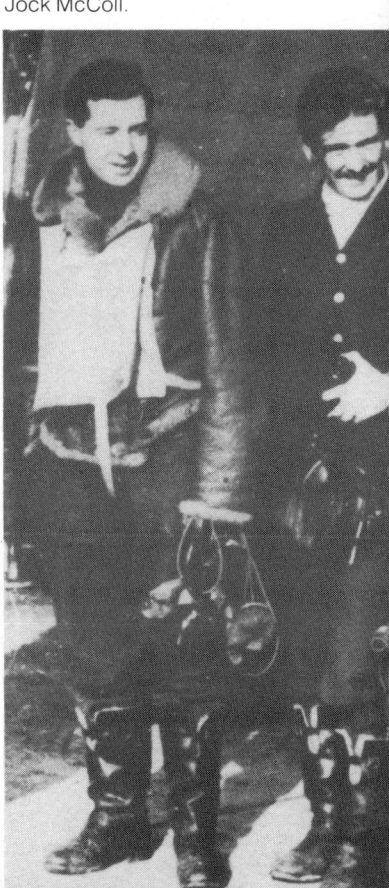

At Ballykelly, Northern Ireland, where Terry spent a brief period, the main runway crossed the line to Londonderry. Here a Liberator waits for a train to go by.

With Wing Commander Charles Drapper, CO of 86 Squadron, just after an off-duty mishap . . ., 'I fell off my bicycle while playing the bag-pipes.'

The crew that sank U-514. From left to right: Second Pilot Ginger Lord, Terry Bulloch, Jock McColl. Sandy Lewis is fourth from the right with navigator Frank Durrant extreme right.

water but only one had re-emerged. This hinted at the other seven having struck home and no submarine built could possibly survive this treatment. One good strike was all that was needed.

Terry Bulloch was never one to let an enemy escape if at all possible. Further encouraging signs immediately appeared, the U-boat could be seen nose down at about 40 degrees with just its aft hydroplanes and propellers aimlessly thrashing clear of the water. These then disappeared, apparently straight down. To the crew it looked 100% sunk without trace. They lacked Terry's intimate knowledge of how strongly the U-boats were built.

To make absolutely sure, Terry now turned to his other weapons. 'No point having them on board and not to use them, is there?' First he levelled off at 500 feet, the prescribed height for the release of his 'Wandering Willie'. This was floated down on a parachute to ensure that it struck the water gently without damage to its sensitive homing mechanism. On impact, the parachute automatically disengaged and the torpedo engine started. To mark the spot, Terry also dropped a smoke flare to burn on the water.

By the time that Terry could get his plane around and back to his flare, an object was seen in the water circling aimlessly in a circle of about 30-40 feet diameter. Sandy Lewis is convinced that this was Wandering Willie, searching in vain for a clue as to which direction to head. It could, however, just have been the rear end of the U-boat pointing perpendicularly down and thrashing about with propellers turning.

To counter any possible suggestion of this kind, Terry made another run and this time dropped all eight depth-charges. These fell slap into the middle of the wandering objects swirl and were followed by a colossal explosion. One way or another Terry was as convinced as he ever had been that this particular U-boat had 'had it'.

The ace killer had done it again. The Admiralty were able to confirm the kill almost at once as Terry had located an Escort Group nearby and had directed it to the scene of his multi-weapons attack. This was no ordinary kill. *U-514* was a Type IXC built at Hamburg. These larger U-boats were prized kills. They had an operational range of 11,000 miles and had sunk ships off Capetown and deep into the Indian Ocean. They also served Doenitz well by acting as supply ships for the smaller U-boats after they had run out of torpedoes (the Type VIIs could only carry 14), fuel or water. Like the other U-boats which Terry Bulloch had sunk, this one also was *Totalverlust* with more than fifty men inside sent to the bottom.

During the Lib's various attacks, efforts had been made to obtain photographic evidence. The sight of those rockets being fired was of special interest. Among the many special additions to this special (overloaded) Lib were a cine camera in the nose, another fitted in the tail and, as usual, Jock McColl had with him the large RAF hand-held camera; an unnecessary bulky item. With this, as the aircraft turned and banked he had endeavoured to snap what pictures he could from the plane's various open gun positions etc. The best shots were expected from the cine and the tail cameras.

All the films were rushed to the photographic section for immediate processing. When done, the crew with all the Top Brass of the Station trooped off to the Station's cinema. They were agog to see what it had looked like in print.

The cine film showed a very clear picture of the tower of the church at the end of the runway when the camera had been switched on for testing purposes and never switched off again! Who was supposed to have switched it off? Various members looked askance at one another. Sergeant Pilot Ginger Lord was junior and naturally was the recipient of most looks. It was only the crew's second operation together: teething troubles? Not in Terry's view. He had no time for excuses.

The film from the tail section showed absolutely nothing at all. The navigator, Frank Durrant, had forgotten to switch it on. He had several other urgent tasks to perform during the attack – snapping out an immediate aircraft position for the wireless operator to flash back to base etc. Like all on board, other than Jock, it was the first time that he had taken part in an attack. More excuses: *not* appreciated by the skipper.

The film from Jock's hand-held camera showed acres of sea but nothing else apart from some nice cloud shots. Terry was not at all amused and the Top Brass went back to their offices wondering why they had wasted their time.

In many respects this was the single most outstanding anti-U-boat attack by a pilot of Coastal Command during the entire war. Within a matter of only a few weeks, a pilot and his crew had carried out a series of successful, difficult and dangerous trials which had resulted in a new kind of weapon being fitted to the Command's principal anti-U-boat plane. He had then proved that the weapon could sink submarines at the first attempt and had guided an Escort Group to the area as additional proof. The only hitch had been the failure to bring back photographic evidence.

Yet if Coastal Command was pleased with this latest chapter of the Terry Bulloch legend, they didn't show it. For the experimental work alone, it would not have been a surprise if Terry Bulloch had been awarded the Air Force Cross (AFC). This award was reserved for meritorious feats in the air *not* carried out in the face of the enemy. It was given to test pilots and the like. For positively sinking a U-boat, it was almost standard to be given a DSO. It was a small price to pay. Even the smaller Type VII required 400,000 man-hours to produce and the Type IXs nearly twice that number. Moreover the crew of 50+ would have spent the best part of a year training in the Baltic. They and the time that they had put in, would be lost forever more.

But Terry and his crew received absolutely nothing. It is difficult to think why this feat was so blatantly ignored. It is possible that, because 'BOAC' had attached himself to 224 Squadron in such an irregular manner, that the system of awards didn't cover this 'posting'. The CO of the unit may have thought that HQ would be making the recommendation and vice versa. It is also possible that HQ found itself in an impossible situation having so recently summarily 'dismissed' the squadron leader from the position of CFI of their Heavy Conversion Unit. Could they now give this same rebel the *unique* distinction of a third DSO? No Coastal Command pilot had ever received the DSO and two Bars. Did the old sores still linger? Those who had been labelled 'Windy buggers' and had heard about it, may still have been smarting. Likewise those who had fought for Terry Bulloch to be allowed to take the Cranwell course only to have him turn down their over-generous offer might still feel their faces red. 'Hell has no fury like a woman scorned'. Maybe Air Marshals felt the same?

When the subject was raised, all Terry would say was, 'They might perhaps have given me, or at least the crew, something. Anyhow, I wasn't doing it for medals.' He is, and always will be, the most genuine of persons but it was obvious that he felt a mite piqued. And who could blame him?

The Bull was more than a 'mite piqued' when months afterwards, the decision was made that Liberators were *not* to be equipped with RPs and those units which were already so equipped would have to remove them. This made him hopping mad.

RPs worked well on a number of aircraft including even the ancient but very honourable Swordfish – the dear old 'Stringbag', that antiquated bi-plane which, with a torpedo, had stopped the mighty *Bismarck*. Several Liberator squadrons were equipped with RPs. They were not always popular with the crews since the extra 'wings' tacked on to the sides to hold the rails for the RPs rather upset the flying balance of a plane which in a dozen other ways had been laden with more and more equipment.

One Liberator unit so equipped was a Polish Squadron, 311. The Poles were well known to be the most brave, almost foolhardy, bunch of pilots in the RAF. Life and death seemed much the same for them, isolated as they were from their loved ones. They knew at first hand what absolute swines some Germans could be and were determined to make them pay for the rape of their country.

Armed with RPs they made swooping dives on anything which looked the slightest like a U-boat but instead of gently easing the Libs out of their dives, the Terry Bulloch way, they hauled the big planes around as if flying fighters. The results were predictable. They so overstressed the structures that some planes had to be declared as 'write-offs' and others as 'severely damaged'. After which the edict went out that Libs were not to carry RPs. Terry was really upset. For one thing he had by then further perfected the weapon and had his 'own' private Lib (the only plane of 'BOAC'!) modified so as to be able to carry the RPs inside the bomb bay on retractable rails.*

After his spectacular beginning with 224 Squadron, Fate seemed to turn against Terry Bulloch. He flew as hard as ever, over 100 hours during several months, but the U-boats failed to appear. He

---

* When blasted off, the sheets of flame almost engulfed the tail gunner 'Absolutely terrifying' in Sandy Lewis's words.

became, in fact, just another frustrated Coastal Command pilot: forever searching but never finding. Bad luck also dogged his flying. When taking off in his overloaded Lib, Terry had the misfortune to run into a flock of seagulls. By skill and keeping his head, he managed to get the damaged aircraft back safely on to the runway several *tons* over its allowable maximum weight. All aboard could so easily have joined the fourteen dead gulls later found dead on the runway.

After his second spell at Boscombe Down (proving that RPs could be carried inside the plane without the flying qualities being adversely affected) Terry, this time in Lib BZ 501 – a Lib V, took himself to Ballykelly in Northern Ireland and was attached to 59 Squadron (Liberators). Northern Ireland had been a previous happy hunting ground so, perhaps 'BOAC' could operate successfully from there.

Not only did he sight no U-boats during his brief spell with 59 Squadron but he suffered the indignity of damaging an aircraft for the first time since 'discovering' two years earlier the low trench left by the workmen at Prestwick. On a flight to show what his own brand of RPs could, and should, be doing, he pulled up the undercarriage a fraction too quickly with the result that the plane collapsed on to its belly and slid to the end of the runway. The bad luck which now seemed to be dogging him was that he had on board a number of senior officers from HQ. The flight was to impress upon them how formidable RPs were. They were not impressed at all.

The Command decided to rub Terry's nose in the mess he had created. They affixed a Red Endorsement in his Log Book, a supreme insult to their most experienced and most successful U-boat hunter. Clearly there was an undeclared war between him and some at HQ. Terry Bulloch would have none of it and by skilful use of a steam kettle wasted no time in promptly removing the insult. There isn't a trace of it now showing! If Bulloch decides to do a thing, he does it properly. The plane was not seriously damaged and was operational again within a week or so.

Finding no pickings with 59 Squadron, Terry next took 'BOAC' to Iceland (by then he appears to have been fighting a purely personal war, taking himself to wherever he fancied and taking with him a personal aircraft). It was from Iceland that he had written his 'Day to Remember' into the history books. In this island, he attached himself to 86 Squadron, another Liberator unit. By then it was April 1944 and Terry had been flying diligently, with three different units, for the best part of eight months with nothing to show for it. 'BOAC' was not turning out well.

By June 1944, almost exactly on D Day – the day when the Allies commenced their recapture of Europe from the German invaders, and during the weeks which followed when Coastal Command achieved the greatest triumph of the war, Terry, with 86 Squadron, was nearly 1,000 miles away in the tip of North Scotland. 86 Squadron had removed itself to Tain in order to hunt for U-boats which were lurking in wait for the Arctic convoys. He therefore missed Coastal's wonderful period when in June 1944 they, with massive Navy help, successfully bottled up the U-boats which had been assembled in large numbers at the adjacent French ports in order to prevent the Allies landing in France.

Every time they attempted to get at the stream of ships heading for the Normandy beaches they were spotted and attacked: day and night. Not one single ship of the many thousands involved on that day was hit by a submarine, nor for weeks thereafter. Doenitz's orders had been to cut into the Allies' shipping lanes 'at all cost'.

One irony of this situation was that, while Terry languished in far away Scotland finding nothing, the squadrons which were finding rich pickings in the Channel area (one aircraft even sank two submarines during a single night's sortie) were, by order, using the attack tactics that Terry had worked out. They were attacking U-boats along, rather than across, their tracks.

Another strange occurrence was that, up at Tain, Terry for reasons unknown was being compelled to use a Liberator that lacked most of the new advantages. The Lib that he took out on several sorties was not even fitted with the ASV Mark III. The earlier Mark II was on board. This was almost useless as, not only was it always relatively ineffective over rough seas but its frequency was known to the enemy and a simple Metox* search receiver had been put on board all U-boats. This warned them that they were

---

* Metox was the name of the French firm assembling this device.

being searched for by this early radar.

In such a plane, Terry was detailed to carry out a search in an area up to the Arctic circle. In Latitude, 72 degrees North, in poor visibility with a sea fog around, his Liberator was detected, first by the noise of its engines, and then visually, by *U-636*. By 1944 U-boats had been almost 'armed to the teeth' and were equipped with a number of anti-aircraft guns mounted in pairs. An additional conning tower had been added to accommodate them, generally referred to as the U-boat's 'band-stand'. Many U-boats were now prepared to fight it out with the planes which were harassing them so continually whenever they dared to surface. *U-636* was one such.

As the Lib was almost on top of the U-boat, it was able to riddle it with accurate fire. Terry's aircraft was hit in both starboard engines and hits were also scored on its starboard rudders. The plane was 900 miles from friendly shores* and beneath were the icy seas, in which a man could live for only minutes. The Bull was in trouble as never before. As usual, Jock McColl was the flight engineer and he and his captain set about taking the immediate actions that alone could save the plane. There was no thought of being able to swing around and attack the U-boat, still surfaced and, clearly, willing to fight it out.

The Liberator had shuddered and rattled upon being hit and almost at once the starboard outer engine began to run down. Both Jock and Terry knew what had to be done. It had to have its propeller stopped and 'feathered' without delay before the hydraulic oil of the sophisticated feathering system drained out. If it couldn't be feathered then the plane had no hope of reaching any base. A windmilling propeller adds enormously to the aircraft's drag. Terry reached forward and hit the feathering button. Everything depended upon the system working. They held their breath. It *had* to work, thank God it did: the propeller slowed and stopped with its blades pointing into the airflow.

Terry had other problems. The plane was not responding normally to its flying controls: yet such response was vital. With

---

* It was only minutes of flying time from occupied Norway but Coastal Command pilots never for a moment considered ditching or landing on or near enemy held territory. They knew that their planes carried secrets which the enemy would love to be able to examine.

No 4 stopped and feathered, the plane had much more power on one side than on the other and was trying to slew itself to starboard. To counter this both Terry and Lord* (each had a set of flying controls linked together) were shoving hard with their left feet to apply maximum rudder but it was the rudder that was not responding normally.

McColl added to the captain's problems by announcing that No 3, the other engine on the starboard side, was also damaged and that, in his view, that, too, should be stopped and its propeller feathered. By winding on maximum rudder trim, the pilots could apply less foot-power to the rudder bars but if No 3 also had to be stopped or, even worse, was allowed to windmill, then they were really in an impossibly perilous position.

Terry was striving, by using the good engines on the port side to gain a little height. Height meant safety. If he had to ditch and, with the crew, take to the dinghies carried for such an emergency, he could do so under better control from a greater height than the low level that the plane had been forced down to by the engine failures. It was a vicious circle. To gain height, he had to 'pour on the power' of the good engines. The increased power made the aircraft slew sideways. If only the rudders would respond better.

'Tail to Captain.'

'Captain answering.'

'Skipper, we've lost a large part of the starboard rudder ... and, captain, I can see bits falling off the starboard engines.'

Jock's voice cut in. His accent was so pronounced that there was never a need for him to identify himself.

'I can't keep No 3 going much longer. We really ought to feather it.'

That would produce an impossible situation.

Terry's calm voice gave the order.

'Not to feather it: not now anyhow! Reduce power on it and see if we can get something useful out of it.'

Bit by bit they struggled upwards. Next decision. Should they send an SOS or 'Mayday' on the wireless. At the height that they were operating and at the distance from base, it was doubtful if *any*

---

* Now Pilot Officer Lord, having been commissioned.

message would be received. It was also important to report the
U-boat and its position. It was a pity that Layton was not in the
crew, he would have done half the necessary actions without even
being asked.

McColl reported that No 4, which they had stopped, was showing
signs of being on fire but luckily the fire blew itself out before it took
hold. By exerting all their strength on the rudder bar, the two pilots
gradually brought the aircraft around to a homewards course.
Slowly – ever so slowly they were winning the battle against gravity.

'OK, we got some height now, I'm feathering No 3 before that
also catches fire.'

With two engines on the same side stopped and half the rudder
lost the plane started for home. The port engines were at near full
power. They were in danger of overheating. If either of them gave
up, all would be lost.

'Right, chaps'. Terry almost seemed to be enjoying himself now
that the immediate crisis was over. 'Lighten the aircraft'. McColl
had gone aft to get a better view of the state of the rudders. The
wireless operator had contacted base and was advising them of their
plight and the U-boat sighting.

The bomb doors were opened and over a ton of depth-charges
went tumbling harmlessly into the sea below. Guns and ammunition
followed: another ton or more lighter. The Lib responded almost at
once and the engines on the port side could at last be throttled back.
Their engine temperature gauge gradually ceased to rise and
eventually fell back and steadied below the red lined maximum.

Terry and Lord were able also to relax their foot-pressures. Both
were fatigued and their leg muscles ached. An added horror was the
increase in noise within the aircraft. The various holes in the
fuselage sang and whistled in the slip-stream; like sirens singing a
sad farewell.

For five long weary hours they battled their way homewards on
two engines and the damaged rudder. It was a feat of physical
endurance. Moments of abject terror weary a man. Some 'age' years
in seconds under supreme stress. This was hours, not seconds.

One of Terry's great charms – and it surprises some who have
only encountered the fierce initial surface of the man, is his grin. It is
a mischievous smile and he uses it when he knows that 'he is being

naughty'. It is easy to imagine that it creased his face all those years before (and they seemed by 1944 to belong to a distant age) when he had dropped the sea-marker on to the spotless foredeck of HMS *Nelson*. There is something in the man that almost compels him to be provocative at times. This was one such moment.

With the problems of the flight largely solved and Tain only minutes of flying time away, Terry found that the track he was making would take him over Scapa Flow, the huge Royal Navy base of the Home Fleet. It was, of course, a prohibited flying area marked by a great splodge of red on all RAF maps. He decided to fly straight through it.

As he explained this action: 'I was bloody tired by then (he had had the most harrowing 16 hours of his life) and they knew I was coming' but the mischievous gleam in his eyes could not be concealed. He knew that he could, and should, have flown the few extra miles around the naval base. Flying over it, in defiance of orders, was the only pleasure that he had had in all that ghastly flight.

Despite the poor visibility and sea-fog, Lord was never subsequently forgiven for not having spotted the U-boat before it had opened fire. The U-boat had been on the starboard side of the aircraft – the side where Lord was supposed to be the look-out. Terry could be a hard man on such occasions and this was one. Had it been on his side and had he been the one who had failed to see it (bad conditions or not), he would have been equally, and brutally, hard on himself.

The log of *U-636* (later sunk by the British ships *Bazeley*, *Drury* and *Bentinck* just a few weeks before the surrender in 1945) has survived. It shows that the U-boat, unusually, first heard, then saw, the plane. Terry, at the time, had reckoned that it, like many U-boats in 1944, had been equipped with their version of radar and had detected him in the poor visibility by such means but it was not so. By the time that *U-636* saw the plane, they had time to train all their guns on it. They also realised, by its unhurried actions, that it had not seen them and was in no position to attack. The U-boat log also confirms that the visibility was poor. (Lord would have loved to have had this confirmed at the time!)

The U-boat captain, Kapitänleutnant Schendel, made a very

modest and accurate claim. Terry himself could hardly have been terser or more faithful to the events. Schendel wrote that he had hit the four-engined plane in the starboard engines and on its rudder: exactly as he had done. That was all. No claim to have shot the aircraft down.

U-636 was one of the U-boats based at Narvik, N. Norway, and the encounter took place within only a few miles of Norway's shores. It was on its eighth war cruise.

By the date (April 1945) when *U-636* fell to the Royal Navy, Terry was 12,000 miles away approaching Auckland, N.Z: in the air, of course; in a Lib, of course; and with the faithful Jock McColl, now a commissioned engineer officer, only a few inches away from him ... of course.

CHAPTER TEN

In Another World

Although the twelve months that Terry Bulloch spent from July 1943 were probably the most disappointing of his wartime career – especially those when 'posted' to 59 and 86 Squadrons, there were a few enjoyable moments. One came at Tain, otherwise his most unhappy station. Terry, for once, decided to 'let his hair down' and arranged to meet his crew in the local for a booze-up. Never one to do things by halves, he made a really good evening of it. Eventually the Balnagowan Hotel closed its doors. By then Terry had learnt that a local piper lived next door. This was great. It struck a responsive chord in his memory. Had he not been the Pipe Major of the Campbell College band?

In no time Terry was pounding on the piper's door. Eventually the poor fellow appeared in his pyjama top and with trousers half on. Terry wanted the loan of his bagpipes. Terry has piercing eyes and when he looks at you and 'suggests' that he wants something, it is hard to refuse him. He would not take 'No' for an answer and eventually the piper, eager to get back to bed, agreed.

After some preliminary tuning, and much encouraged by the crew, Terry marched up and down playing Irish airs with the crew marching proudly behind him. This was too much for the worthy inhabitants of Tain: to be awakened from their sleep in the middle of the night by someone playing Irish tunes in their Scottish High Street. The local bobby was roused. The defender of the laws fortunately took a tolerant view of the proceedings. During wartime the police were apt to be even more tolerant about the 'boys in blue' than in peacetime. Terry and his crew, as was usual in wartime when petrol for private use was virtually non-existent, had cycled to the local hostelerie. By tact and persuasion, the policeman managed to persuade the inebriated crew to wobble homewards as best they could. The incident may have been behind a photograph which the CO of the squadron, Wing Commander C. Drapper, has preserved which is reproduced in this book. It shows Terry and him enjoying a beer with the former's arm in a sling.

'What happened there, Terry?'

'Oh, that ... I fell off my bicycle while playing the bag-pipes.'

Yet he could be tough with his crew. As Sandy Lewis recalls: 'Terry was one of the finest men I have ever known. Familiar with his crew but strict. On one occasion, when he considered that we had returned from leave late, he made us clean down the aircraft with buckets of petrol. You can have no idea how cold petrol can be!' It was entirely against orders to use petrol in this way and, equally, for an officer (such as Sandy was) to be ordered to clean down an aircraft but crew spirit and Terry's personality won the day. Another of Terry's habits, when not flying or catching up with Intelligence, was to play games of 'Volunteer Snooker'. With his eyesight, he was a demon potter and, as usual, he took the game with seriousness. The officers in his crew were given little chance to say him nay. He was a hard man to refuse. He liked his snooker.

Earlier when with 224 Squadron, he had twice found dinghies with survivors in them. This, too, made life worthwhile. Air battles over the Bay of Biscay had become frequent and the losers were apt to end up 'in the drink'. On the first occasion, the dinghy contained three airmen and Terry probably saved their lives by guiding destroyers to their aid. On the other occasion, the occupants appeared to be Germans but Terry dropped water and supplies nonetheless.

When it was put to Terry that he appears to have mellowed towards his sworn enemies, the rebuttal was swift:

'Not at all. Not a bit. I just wasn't *sure* that they were Jerries.' If compassion had entered his soul, he most certainly wasn't going to admit it. It was said without a hint of his mischievous chuckle but the 'wicked' glint in his eyes was there. Did he mean it? Could anyone tell? Did Terry himself know?

Terry was never caught by the Ju88* long-range fighters which, in quite large numbers patrolled the Bay in groups and pounced upon any Coastal Command aircraft they found. They were faster and

---

* More rarely Coastal Command pilots were also engaged by the more formidable Me110s and 210s which were much faster: as the author knows only too well!

more manoeuverable than the laden anti-submarine planes. Terry twice spotted formations in the distance. Not even he was prepared to tangle with a flight of fighters and, since he had sighted them first, he managed to evade them. The low clouds under which so many weary hours of 'bumps' had to be endured came to the rescue of many a Coastal plane.

On another occasion, Terry, off the coast of Spain, came so close to the shore that shore batteries opened up at him. Thereafter he stayed a more legal distance. 'Pity', remarked one crew member, 'I was enjoying peering at the senoritas sunning themselves on the beaches.'

Postings seemed to follow close behind the most memorable events of his career. Within a week of his encounter with *U-636*, Terry was posted, not just from 86 Squadron (where he had never been happy) but also out of the Command. It was not that this harrowing 'dice with death' had shaken him (he went out again two days later on another 15-16 hour patrol up towards the Arctic Circle) but, more likely, that Coastal Command simply couldn't find the proper niche for this 'odd-ball' who insisted upon flying and who, despite his rank of squadron leader and vast experience as an operational pilot, had no interest in higher command.

Pilots with his seniority were normally preserved and rested at regular intervals; either being temporarily 'grounded' by being given a desk job in HQ or by being sent to the calmer waters of flight instruction at an OTU. Group had tried the latter and were disinclined to repeat the experiment. They had allowed 'BOAC' to do it *his* way for a year or so. After the initial success of the sinking of *U-514*, the results had been disappointing. He didn't ever seem to want a rest from flying: the recuperative period that almost all others seemed to need in order to rebuild their strength, and recover their nerve, for further operational flying.

A transport squadron had been formed at Lyneham, Gloucs, to operate one of the transport versions of the Liberator now being produced. This version was known as the C 87C. It flew mail, urgently wanted freight and VIPs to almost anywhere: Russia, Cairo, India, West Africa, etc, etc. The unit also had a few Yorks. Its Libs were known as the Liberator Express aircraft.

Terry Bulloch joined the unit on 29 August 1944 and without further ado promptly settled down to the new task. He had been given a quite different crew but by a classic piece of wangling, somehow included Jock McColl.*

His first flight was to Gibraltar and thence on to Rabat. Having a day off here and wishing to get to know his crew better, they all went to explore. While doing so, they encountered a senior Army S.P. officer, as officious as he was exalted in rank. Terry was correctly dressed. From childhood onwards, he has always been neat and well groomed but he was not actually *wearing* his fore-and-aft forage cap. It was tucked under his squadron leader's shoulder epaulettes. The officious SP hauled Terry up and started to dress him down in front of his crew. He probably was upset at finding officers and sergeants mixing so freely together: maybe, he had seldom met an RAF crew off-duty? For whatever reason, it seems an unnecessary act on his part. As he was about to find out, it was perpetrated at the wrong person!

Terry had previously tossed one Army SP officer into a swimming pool and if there had ben one at hand, it is more than likely that history would be repeating itself. In no uncertain terms, Terry told the SP (McColl thinks he was a colonel) to 'get lost' and to 'get his arse off his cushy job and to go and do some fighting instead of messing about with those who were trying to win the war.' The officer was most upset! Terry was threatened with dire retribution. 'The matter will be taken up at the highest level. You've not heard the last of this.' Terry was quite unabashed and informed the irate Special that 'he couldn't care less what he did.'

Perhaps Terry's frustration at being posted so far away from where the heat of the battle was raging had boiled over? Or was the Army officer just too envious at the sight of an RAF officer wearing the ribbons of a double DSO and double DFC while he was stuck with a police job not of his own choosing?

At the best of times the Army, with its centuries-old traditions, honours and habits, seldom found itself on the same frequency with the RAF – that less formal, newer, much more brash Service. Certainly the Army never understood what it meant to be a part of an RAF crew: that closely-knit mixture of officers and sergeants who, while on Ops, ate, lived and died together bound so inexorably by ties of unswerving loyalty and mutual reliance.

* McColl had to be transferred from Coastal to Transport Command and thence to Terry's crew.

Normally, when not on Ops (or training), the crew separated into their respective Messes and saw little of each other but the camaraderie was always there and at suitable opportunities both 'sides' willingly and eagerly removed the official barriers that separated them. Intelligent commanding officers were prepared to close their eyes to such fraternisation. They knew it was good for crew morale, good for the squadron spirit.

Flights to other places followed: to the Azores (also 'taken over', much as Iceland had been but with less local distaste), Karachi, Malta, Calcutta, Allahabad, Tobruk, Naples, etc. Between flights, Terry also found time to attend a radio-navigation course at Prestwick.

Although he had turned his back on the prestigious Cranwell Administration course, he never missed half a chance to attend any, and every, course that might keep him up-to-date with the latest developments in flying and navigation. He never pretended, for all his experience, that he knew it all. If meteorology, radio-aids or navigation courses were around, he somehow got to attend and invariably took the course with seriousness: to pass with honours. Towards flying, his attitude was 100% professional.

The C 87 Libs he was flying have been described* as 'the worst B-24s ever built.' Like almost all Libs, it was, as war progressed, tons over its original designed weight. It was reluctant to leave the ground and wallowed laboriously until, as fuel was consumed, it became more manageable. Terry had been flying overloaded Libs for years and didn't notice anything much different. It gave him no problem.

By 1945 it was obvious to all, except perhaps to Adolf Hitler, that the war in Europe could only end one way: and soon. Pilots with Terry's love of flying and who had the forethought to be able to look to the future, were casting around to see how they could best equip themselves for a career in post-war aviation. It was equally obvious that the great advances in aviation that had been made during the war (vide flying the Atlantic, for instance) would result in an explosion of civil aviation such as the world had never seen. Many

---

* By Ernest K. Gann, author and later senior Pan-Am pilot.

Focke-Wulf FW 200c (Condor) over the grey waters of the Atlantic amidst typical leaden skies. Wartime pictures of this aircraft, which located Allied convoys and co-ordinated with U-boat command, had the aerials of its airborne radar painted out as also was the case with Terry's Liberator Is. Both sides regarded this as a top secret device.

Interior of a Type VIIc U-boat showing the cramped and insanitary conditions in which the 44-man crew had to exist for up to six weeks on end with little or no water for washing and with the smell and taste of diesel oil permeating every fibre. The lack of beards indicates that photograph was taken on a training exercise.

Five crews of 120 Squadron were awarded South Atlantic medals after the Falkland Islands Campaign 1983. Squadron Leader Terence Malcolm Bulloch, DSO and bar, DFC and bar, pictured *(above)* at the ceremony and *(below)* presenting a medal.

pilots would want to be a part of this: only the best would be chosen. Terry Bulloch had acquired vast experience already but he saw a chance to obtain even more. Somehow he got to know about a squadron which almost no one in Britain had ever heard about; either then or since.

At the time he was based in Montreal with 45 Group. He had got himself posted there from Lyneham. For one thing, it was offering an advanced radio-range (beam) navigation course. He had previously passed the one at Prestwick but realised that the North American way of 'flying the beam' was more advanced. He duly passed this course with a rating of 'Up to good Airline Standard'; a real feather in his cap for the scramble for jobs that would follow at war's end. 45 Group and Montreal were old stomping grounds for Terry. It was this Group which had arranged the early Trans-Atlantic flights and the Return Ferry Service of the real BOAC.

Terry had mastered all that Montreal could offer: and, thanks to his spell at Lyneham, the routes to Europe, Africa and India as well. As soon as he heard about 231 Squadron, he reckoned that this was 'right up his alley'. This almost unknown RAF Unit was based in San Diego, Southern California, and flew a transport version of the Liberator all the way to Auckland, New Zealand, by way of Hawaii, Canton Islands and Fiji. It terminated the run at Sydney. It spanned the Pacific and, although the war in Europe had ceased, the fight was still raging with fury in that area.

By some unique method (that wing commander Irish friend in HQ must have been a genius!) Terry got himself posted to this 'one-off' RAF Squadron, based almost within sight of Mexico.

It satisfied a number of wants. It gave Terry a chance to fly and navigate across an ocean that he had not mastered. It enabled him, ever active, to get closer to where the only remaining action of the war was taking place and it enabled him, always staunchly British to be 'Showing the Flag' in a theatre of war almost entirely dominated by the Americans. Terry always got on well with the Americans, but was never a great Yank lover. He had read deeply into British history and was proud of his British (but never English) heritage. His directness always went down well with the US personnel he met. He left it at that.

The aircraft used by 231 Squadron were the (Liberator) RY-3s. It was a version that originally had been ordered by the US Navy. It was the only version to be fitted with a huge single tail. All the others had the familiar twin rudders, looking like a pair of dustbin-lids. Like the wallowing C 87Cs, the RY-3s carried up to 20 passengers but had plenty of space for urgent freight as well. It was strictly a VIP run.

The Liberators all cruised at a (then) high speed of about 250 mph at altitude, thanks to their turbo-supercharged Pratt & Whitney engines, but even so, the flight time to Sydney was about 38 hours with the longest leg of the journey – the initial San Diego to Hawaii one, accomplished in about twelve hours. It was a tiring schedule but Terry never seemed to tire when in the air: also he had a reliable Flight Engineer Officer on board, the ever present Flying Officer Jock McColl, now commissioned. Jock had come a long way since being discovered in the hangars at Nutts Corner when a Fitter 2(E). All along that route he had sat only inches away from the same Ulster skipper.

The Pacific weather is generally kind to aviators. The Lib was a good one. The job was, in the Bull's estimation, 'a piece of cake'. It didn't seem to annoy him that his commanding officer was a Squadron Leader Patrick – a pilot with far less experience and one, probably, junior to him. Rank and promotion never meant much to Terry Bulloch. When June came around his annual assessment was, as usual, 'Exceptional'. This meant more, especially as it covered both piloting and navigation.

By then Terry was ready and waiting for the years of peace which stretched ahead. In all, he had passed with distinction, three advanced radio-navigation courses of the kind that would benefit a civil pilot. He had flown literally all over the world and spanned its greatest oceans. While a part of him still wanted to continue to serve the RAF – his boyhood dream – he was realist enough to acknowledge, that he and they didn't quite fit.

In answer to Terry's requests to know whether his Short Service Commission, which originally had been for four years (from 1937), with six more on the Reserve, could be extended indefinitely, the best that was offered was a suggestion (no more) of an Intermediate Term Commission: one of eleven years.

Terry by 1945 was aged nearly thirty. An unconfirmed offer of a career which would see him 'turned out to grass' at aged forty or forty-one was hardly attractive.

The Civil Aviation field beckoned. The sheer statistics of his qualifications were formidable:

Total hours: 4568

Hours on Liberators: 1721

Operational trips: 350

Operational hours: 2059

If nothing else, these figures proved that he was a 'survivor' and, in aviation, this meant much. Some pilots seem to be born with an innate extra 'sense' that kept them out of serious trouble. Others, excellent pilots in other ways, lacked it and paid the price in war.

The hours flown with the RAF alone were probably unique. They must surely have exceeded the totals flown by any other wartime pilot? His decorations were also formidable but in civil aviation they would count for little. The hours would speak louder. As would also the navigation courses which he had bothered to find time to take and successfully passed. This would separate him from the other 'press on regardless' aces of the RAF.

Terry naturally set his sights in civil aviation on BOAC. He had worked with them, on and off, for years and had crossed the Atlantic with BOAC as crewmen several times. He knew them and, more importantly, they knew him: and knew him at his best. The Atlantic Ferry organization were well aware that here was an exceptional pilot who never had needed booze or blondes in order to retain his nerve and zest for flying. They probably did not know of his occasional outbursts of bravado when, for instance, he had chased that Hun on the bicycle down the streets of Ijmuiden or when he had illuminated half Hampshire in defiance of the FW190s in the area.

The only bar to the swift and natural post-war 'marriage' between BOAC and Coastal Command's own 'BOAC' was that Terry couldn't get himself de-mobilised. Being so far away from Britain, his papers were delayed. He had to spend many a month cooling his heels awaiting his release. For once his Irish pal in HQ didn't turn up the trumps. Perhaps he wasn't there any more? Being the smart character he appears to have been, maybe he had made sure of his own de-mobilisation first!

While he was waiting to be released, Terry passed yet another navigation course and was able to add to his impressive list of qualifications the 'RAFs Navigation Warrant'. For one, to whom navigation never came easily because he was never naturally dexterous with figures, his long list of navigational passes does him credit.

Although he was 'late' in joining BOAC and lost out some valuable places of seniority (always important with the major Airlines), he was taken on direct as a captain, an almost unique experience and one which put him a big jump ahead of those who had been accepted only as First Officers (BOAC's title for second pilots).

It is no co-incidence that a pilot as keen as he was on meteorology, became, at war's end, engaged to a charming young WAAF Officer who worked in an RAF Met Office. She, too, was Ulster Irish and had lived her early life, literally, just around the corner from Malone Park where young Malcolm, Yvonne and big brother Larmor had so happily played. A Protestant daughter of an Army Colonel, it was almost a Barbara Cartland match although their tastes were different. She was as mad about horses as he had always been about aircraft and in the postwar days it was unusual to see her pretty little figure in anything other than jodpurs.

If BOAC had not taken Terry on, then almost every other airline in the world would have done: not that Terry would have relished flying for a non-British outfit.

So ended the wartime career of Coastal Command's most celebrated, most decorated, most successful anti-submarine pilot. It had its controversial moments (as the Army SPs could verify!) and for the last three years he hardly, if ever, sighted the enemy but by then he had done more than enough. He had shown the way and others in the Command had followed. By war's end the Lib was the top U-boat killer in the Command with the resuscitated 120 Squadron, formed in the mud of Nutts Corner, heading the list with sixteen confirmed kills, four by Squadron Leader T.M. Bulloch.

Britain would be a poorer place without the Terry Bullochs of this world. Britain might never exist at all. As *both* sides found out 1939/45, when the Bull set his sights on a target, he is a mighty hard man to stop.

Epilogue

Terry Bulloch's career as a civil pilot was all that was expected of him. He flew as much or more than any other pilot. He never had difficulty in mastering any of the planes he had to handle. He would have nothing to do with positions of authority which his seniority opened up for him and his smooth accident-free flying record was punctuated by the occasional provocative quirk.

Terry Bulloch always had a short fuse, especially where inefficiency in the air was concerned. The author and he were of almost the exact same seniority (both having been taken on as captains upon demobilisation) and on occasions flew as captain and first officer in the same plane: sometimes he would be in command, at others it would be the other way round. Terry's blasting at my inefficiency as a first officer (an unfamiliar role) could be withering. I could see why some juniors were almost terrified by him. But such outbursts were short-lived. Almost within minutes of my being 'torn off a mighty strip', Terry would be suggesting that we went golfing or swimming together, if time allowed it, at wherever it was that we had stopped for the night! He said what he thought. He could live no other way.

Terry was privileged, right from the outset, to join BOAC's prestigious Trans-Atlantic Service. Not only was this BOAC's premier route, and one which, at the time, only the pre-war civil pilots operated (the so-called Atlantic Barons) but for the first few years after the war, it meant being based in Montreal away from all the privations of Britain,* and receiving substantial extra pay and allowances.

BOAC knew about Terry and he knew about them. It was the right and obvious spot for him and he at once settled down among the elite holding his own. By his usual hard work, he soon passed

* Rationing of food, clothes and petrol was at its very strictest immediately *after* the war ended.

the top civil navigational examination and became a 'First Class Navigator'. A Master Pilot's Certificate followed. There was no higher qualification.

From crudely converted Liberators BOAC rapidly progressed to a handful of early Constellations, thence to the remarkable double-decker Boeing Stratocruisers – the Boeing 377. Pan-Am and BOAC ruled the Atlantic in these comfortable, but difficult to handle planes, for many years. Eventually they gave way to the DC 7Cs and then to the big Boeing Jets, starting with the wonderful B-707. Terry took all these in his stride.* He was not alone in regarding Boeing as the supreme civil aircraft manufacturer. The built in additional strength of their planes impressed him as a pilot.

Before long BOAC had opened up routes to every corner of the globe. Terry Bulloch, being the conservative person he is, made no attempts to widen his horizon. He had done all that in wartime. He liked flying the Atlantic even after it became relatively easy to do so and a far more difficult task than in the late 1940s and 1950s when the planes lacked the fuel for a non-stop journey. He liked it so he stayed with it. Had he wanted, he could have been given instructional roles with the Corporation; check pilot or, later, flight managerial positions. All such posts would have meant less flying. They were not for him.

What of Jock McColl? He soon learnt that Terry was with BOAC. His demobilisation came later. By then he was a flight lieutenant. As soon as he could, he followed Terry into the Corporation; naturally as an Engineer Officer, and in no time was flying in his accustomed position; at times a few inches away from Terry Bulloch over the ocean they had got to know so well in wartime.

I am indebted to another Flight Engineer of BOAC, Johnny Winston, for two of the many Bulloch stories which distinguished this captain from the others. Terry was never a great respecter of high personages and most certainly never one to go 'crawling' in order to curry favours. Winston writes:

As a young and impressionable flight-engineer, I was in awe of Terry whose reputation went ahead of him like a bow-wave. He

---

* The Atlantic division was given the best American planes and first crack at them with Terry often helping to deliver them to the UK.

never suffered fools gladly and demanded the best of everyone. It made me determined to give him my best. His manner was somewhat forebidding ... but I firmly believe that there was no malice in him. He was without doubt a WW II hero and a figure to look up to but whether his caustic bearing should have been projected into civil life is another matter. The greatest tribute I could pay Terry is that he was one of the best and, more importantly, the safest pilot it was my pleasure to fly with. I felt that whatever unpleasant conditions, weather or technical, we might encounter, Terry would get us out of it.

On one occasion we were late starting from New York due to an unserviceable ground starter truck and, during the long taxi to the take off, Sir Miles Thomas (the much publicised Chairman of BOAC), who happened to be on board sent the Chief Steward up with a note to Terry suggesting that the passengers might like to know the reason for the late departure. Terry didn't want to hear the request. The steward retreated without so much a hint of a reply only to reappear a few moments later to repeat the request. Terry turned on the unsuspecting steward and bellowed: 'You get back and tell Sir Miles with my compliments that I'm in charge of this bloody aircraft and not him and to mind his own business!'

'In those exact words, sir?'

'Yes.'

It is not everyone who would have been so outspoken to his own Chairman. Regardless of rank or position, Terry says what he thinks and on that occasion I believe him to have been right.

On another occasion Johnny Winston recalls that he happened to notice among the passengers, Shelley Berman, a famous American comedian, Shelley had made a name for himself by a cruelly witty skit of an airline captain addressing his passengers. Some thought that it had put civil aviation back by quite a few years. It lampooned the likes of Terry. Winston continues:

Rather daringly, I asked Terry if we could have him up on the flight deck after we had got going and all was squared away. Terry replied in his usual gruff manner that he didn't want passengers on his flight deck. It was therefore with considerable surprise that, when Shelley Berman appeared at the open flight deck door, Terry turned around in his seat and invited him in. Mr Berman made himself at home in the jump seat at the captain's elbow and announced his gratitude especially he was admitting as he had done so much to mock our profession. To my surprise Terry then asked if Shelley would like to address the passengers and handed him the Public Address microphone, whereupon Shelley Berman, with the plane being half way over the Atlantic heading for Britain, announced: 'Good evening, ladies and gentlemen, this is your captain speaking. We're cruising at 35,000 feet and expect to arrive at Cincinatti, Ohio, in 35 minutes time. Prizes will be given to the first three passengers alighting from the aircraft but we respectfully request that you wait until the aircraft has stopped rolling on the runway before you commence competing. Thank you and out!

Some passengers thought that they had boarded the wrong flight: others were convinced that the pilot had lost his marbles and that they were in the hands of some nut. It took the cabin crew quite a while to assure the passengers that it was all a joke and that Shelley Berman was on board. Most were amused but one was sufficiently annoyed to write to the *Evening Standard* suggesting that Captain Bulloch of BOAC should know better than to present himself as an impresario for the benefit of Shelley Berman's publicity. That passenger was not amused: neither was BOAC and poor old Terry was blamed and, I think, reprimanded.

The Bulloch provocative spirit, which had reared its head once or twice in wartime, seems compelled to break out on rare occasions. Although Terry, himself, would be the last person on earth to admit it, the signs are that beneath that formidable manner, a light-hearted person lurks.

When BOAC turned into British Airways Terry went on flying just the same. When an early retirement scheme was proposed, he ignored it. When the Jumbo Jet, the Boeing 747, arrived, he converted to it and went on crossing the Atlantic as diligently as before. Eventually he reached the age when British Airways were compelled to retire him. By then he had flown over six million miles and, post war, had crossed the 'Fishpond' 1,113 times: probably more often than any other British pilot; and always without cause for alarm (Shelley Berman excepted!) for his tens of thousands of passengers. On many such crossings, his flight-engineer was Jock McColl although none of the customers at the back were aware that they were in the hands of the most outstanding of all Coastal teams.

For most pilots this would have been more than enough flying, especially when compounded with his unique number of wartime hours and operational trips. But not for Terry. Although deemed (by Industrial agreement) 'too old' for British Airways, he found himself eligible to fly for the Portuguese National Airline, TAP and promptly joined that outfit. Here he immediately took command of a Boeing 707 and carried on flying the Atlantic, much as before. The step-down from the Jumbo 747 to the smaller and older 707 didn't seem to worry him at all. Appearances and titles always meant little to him. As a young RAF pilot he had had all the honoured glory that any pilot could have wished for.

At much the same time as his switch from British to Portuguese National airlines, he became a widower. Although he set up his abode in, or near, Lisbon, he retained his house in England (naturally the same one as he had lived in for years: he was never one to change a good thing) largely because he had a much-loved dog and he considered it only fair, since it was impractical for him to take the dog to Portugal, to allow the dog, with a housekeeper, to continue its existence in surroundings that were familiar. Loyalty has always been a hall-mark of the Bull. The dog had served him well. Why should he not reciprocate? When finally retired as a pilot for good, he worked almost as hard at his golf as he had done at flying and at aged seventy is no mean performer*. As with other things that matter to him, he is in this hobby fiercely loyal to his Denham Golf Club. It is not any more 'on his doorstep' but he retains membership and will vigorously maintain that it can not be surpassed by any other. 'No greens are as good as Denham's greens!'

It was on this course that he once attacked me verbally. After having sportingly, and helpfully, pointed out some unseen hazard to me (unfamiliar with the course), he announced:

---

* In 1983 he won the RAF Golf Society's Veterans Trophy.

'You're a rotten bastard!'

'What have I done now, Terry?' I knew him too well to be abashed at this unexpected outburst. At the time we were both Senior BOAC Captains.

'They've made you ruddy well senior to me in the Seniority List.'

This was true. This all important 'pecking order' list had, not for the first time, been adjusted. Originally I had been placed above Terry* then it was amended so that he was above me and now it was being amended back to its original. There was nothing I could do about it. My thoughts were interrupted.

'Now, be careful old chap, there is a bunker you can't see from where you are: it's on the right. (Pause) You're a rotten bastard!'

Doubtless Terry will rant and rage about some passages of this book. Terry who has read so much British history (he has read Churchill's massive account of the war twice) deserves his own place in that history and it would be wrong not to tell the tale of Terence Malcolm Bulloch DSO and Bar, DFC and Bar as honestly as it is: warts and all. He is as he is and thousands of Britons sleep more soundly because of it: whether they be those who once stood in peril with Hitler only a 'stone's throw' away from our shores: whether they be those who depended, during the critical years, for supplies from across the world or whether they be those who later stepped from their airliners safe and sound after another uneventful journey.

Terry has found happiness anew with his Canadian wife, Linda. He keeps himself wonderfully fit and, ever active, applies himself diligently to a part-time job. He also harbours an ambition to get around a golf course, preferably Denham's, in less strokes than his age. Being the man he is, I wouldn't bet against it.

Wing Commander McBratney, his CO when together they put 120 Squadron on the map and the U-boats to rout, once described him as: 'A living legend.' Few have ever said it better.

---

* Due solely to the fact that he had to wait (in the Pacific) to be demobilised. We were both taken on direct as captains.

German U-boats destroyed by Allied ships and aircraft during World War II

Destroyed by ships alone

By British ships 206
By American ships 37
Shared by British & American ships 3
By Submarines (all but 2 British) 21
By mines laid by ships & submarines 9
Total 276

Destroyed by aircraft alone

By British aircraft 195
By American aircraft 48
Shared by British & American aircraft 2
By British Carrier aircraft 14
By American Carrier aircraft 29
By British bombing of ports 22
By American bombing of ports 40
By mines laid by British aircraft 16
TOTAL 366

Another 93 were lost by causes largely unknown. The Russians sank a few (7), some were lost in accidents and some were scuttled. But a number were lost for no known reason. Since a surface ship always knew almost for sure if it had or had not sunk the U-boat it was attacking from overhead, a presumption is that aircraft, which had no means of checking what was happening beneath the waves, probably accounted for quite a few more 'kills'.

A total of 48 were destroyed by the combined actions of ships and aircraft and are not included in the above figures. British aircraft, mostly from Coastal Command, were involved in 35 of these 'kills'.

Some experts consider that only 781 were destroyed: Others 785. It is an indication of the difficulties of assessing losses of underwater craft.

By the end of 1941 the Navy had sunk 40 but the RAF only 4: an indication of the state of Coastal Command's unpreparedness for anti-U-boat operations. The Americans had not by then entered the Battle of the Atlantic.

The Tale of *U-254*

By normal reckoning there would be no doubt whatever about the fate of *U-254*. It was attacked and sunk by Squadron Leader T.M. Bulloch on 'The Day to Remember', 8 December 1942; his first attack of that epic flight. After the attack, oil and wreckage were observed by the crew. This included something which attracted a flock of seagulls which appeared to be feasting upon something thrown up by the explosions of the six depth-charges. Terry Bulloch guided a Norwegian corvette to the scene. The ship observed the oil and wreckage plus bodies in the water. By Aldis Lamp, it signalled the circling plane. One message was 'You have killed him.' Nothing could be more conclusive.

Confirmation came from the Naval Operations Intelligence Centre. Commander Winn had noted that *U-254* which he knew was in the location of the attack 'disappeared' for ever on that day. Post-war Coastal Command records show that B120 on 8 December 1942 sank *U-254*.

Some years later Grand Admiral Karl Doenitz published his 'Diaries' (which were really notes). In these he states that: 'As he had so often feared, on the night of December 8 1942, two of the 22 U-boats shadowing Convoy HX 217 had collided. *U-221* accidentally rammed *U-254* and sank it. The crew of *U-221* observed about 30 bodies in the water wearing life jackets and escape gear but reported that, due to the state of the sea, they had only been able to pick up four: a Petty Officer and three ratings.'

The conflicting accounts aroused correspondence. Doenitz was an honourable man and Terry had never been one to attempt to 'pad' or exaggerate his reports: quite the opposite. Terry himself got in touch with the naval historian, Captain D.V. Peyton Ward who, with another RN Captain, Stephen Roskill, was writing an official war history of RAF Operations in the Maritime War. Captain Peyton

Ward's letter to Terry Bulloch, (reproduced in full at the end of this Appendix) clearly indicates that Bulloch had accounted for *U-254*. His words: 'It was your attack which sank *U-254*' are underlined by him.

That again would appear to be the end of the matter. However some years later, officials at the Ministry of Defence, Naval History Section, examined the log of *U-221* and concluded that *U-254* had indeed been rammed by *U-221* and had sunk as a result. A further complication is that the author examined a German publication *Die Deutschen U-Boote* 1939-45 by Otto Mielke which (when translated) states:

U-254 Kapitänleutnant Hans Gilardone. On 8 December 1942 in North Atlantic off Greenland. During an attack on a convoy was rammed by U-boat 410 and after surfacing was bombed by British Aircraft. 6 men saved. Captain killed.'

Corroboration for this is to be found in *U-Boat Losses* in World War II published by the Naval History Division, Office of the Chief of Naval Operations, Washington, DC, 1963, in which the following information is given.

Date	U-Boat and Captain	Position	Aircraft
12/10/42	U-597 – Böpst	56 50'N 28 05'W	H/120
5/10/42	U-132 – Vogelsang	5808'N 33 13'W	H/120
8/12/42	**U-254 – Gilardone**	**57 25'N 35 19'W**	**B/120**
8/7/43	U-514 Aufferman	43 37'N 08 59'W	R/224

Unless the 4 (or 6) survivors can be found and questioned, it is difficult to correlate these various accounts. What seems beyond question is that Terry Bulloch *did* deliver a devastating attack on a U-boat. McColl took photographs of the huge oil slick which ensued. Terry *did* call up the corvette *Potentilla*. This vessel *did* inform him that he had sunk the submarine. All this evidence was compiled at the time of the attack, more than 40 years ago. There are also the seagulls feasting upon something edible and, of course, the official Coastal Command records. Perhaps it is best to quote Captain Peyton Ward's letter in full. It is dated 24 November 1971.

Dear Bulloch;

As you know I was engaged between 1946 and 1960 in writing the history of all RAF Operations in the Maritime War (Bomber, Coastal and Fighter). Naturally the bulk of these were performed by Coastal Command. Of these last the most voluminous were against German U-boats, both in the transit areas and around convoys. To be of any value in estimating the results of such operations, it was necessary to check British claims against German records and vice versa. This was made possible by our possession (through post war capture) of the very extensive German U-boat operational records, U-boat Logs and Admiral Doenitz's personal day to day War Diary. Through my personal contacts with Commander Saunders (in whose charge at the Admiralty were the German records), I was able among other things, to form at the Air Historical Branch a large chart of the Atlantic on which I could plot daily positions (either signalled from the U-boat or estimated by Doenitz) of all U-boats at sea at any period of the war.

Having roughly explained this, I should mention that I also worked with Captain Roskill and most of the accounts in the Official History which refer to RAF were based on my research and operational history.

Now to come to Convoy HX 217. In the early days of December 1942 this convoy was being pursued by 22 U-boats but was receiving powerful air escort notably by 120 Squadron. On 8th, a particularly effective attack was delivered by B/120 resulting in the appearance of copious fuel oil, some wooden debris and some dead bodies. All these were confirmed not only by photographs but by the Norwegian Corvette *Potentilla* (K214) who was guided to the area by signals from B/120. When writing up this episode, I had no hesitation in labelling *U-254* as the victim as her plotted position was the only U-boat near the position given by B/120, and confirmed by *Potentilla*.

In due course this result was included in the Official History. However later I learnt from the Admiralty Foreign Document Section that an interesting sequel had occurred. It appears that the depth-charge attack by B/120 had mortally wounded *U-254* and the crew were endeavouring to claw their way out of the conning tower of the foundering submarine when the second in command (still inside the boat) decided to make a desperate attempt to save the boat. He shut the conning tower hatch and together with the remainder of the crew went down with her. Meanwhile the CO, another junior officer and several ratings perished on the surface amid the oil and wreckage and were duly found by *Potentilla* on her arrival.

Extraordinary to relate the survivors in the U-boat managed finally to control her downwards dive, to temporarily plug the worst leaks and regain the surface some hours later. She staggered eastwards for a long time but it was obvious that she wouldn't last long and the OIC risked a W/T shortwave call for help. Luckily for them this was picked up by another U-boat fairly close to. Again fortune favoured them and a rendez-vous was effected but only just in time. The remainder of the crew scrambled aboard while the stricken *U-254* finally foundered.

Having regard to the end result there seems no necessity to alter the assessment in either Roskill's Official History of RAF Operations. *It was your attack which sank U-254.*

It is possible that in a general covering report of U-boat operations circulated among U-boat Captains and officers of the U-boat service (at the time) the loss of *U-254* was given as collision for propaganda purposes to minimise the growing dismay among them regarding the lethality of air attacks. It must be remembered that in 90% of cases when a U-boat was sunk by depth-charge attack, the Captain had no means of reporting the fact that he was being attacked let alone his fate. All that the German bases could be certain of was his non-arrival in port in due course.

I must make it clear to you that the above story is from growing inaccurate memory. The U-boat at the rendez-vous may well have been *U-221*. I cannot remember. All my 5 volumes of RAF operations are in the archives of Air Historical branch together with my detailed research and extracts from the *contemporary* German reports of U-boat Logs. *Subsequent* German resumés and policy circulations are, in my opinion, of no use in establishing the facts *at the time they actually occurred*.

In this particular story the key witness must be the Log of

*U-221** for this cruise which may still be in the Admiralty Foreign Document Section Archives.

Yours sincerely

D.V. Peyton Ward.

Such a letter takes a lot of disbelieving being, as it is, written by a distinguished Historian: one from a different Service even.

There are certain puzzling aspects about the fate of U-254. Why for instance was the CO among the first to have abandoned the damaged craft? This was not in accord with the German naval practice. By all accounts, their U-boat Service was an honourable one†. Also if, as the *U-221* story asserts, there were 30 men in the sea, why were only 4 picked up? The Germans were excellent sailors and it does not seem all that difficult to rescue men from their low slung decks. Also why were the men allegedly wearing *escape* gear as well as life jackets if the U-boat had not, as *U-221* reports, been attacked.

Above all else, if *U-254* was, as Captain Peyton Ward declares, the only U-boat in that immediate position (a position verified by both

---

* The author had a quick glimpse at this Log which *does* refer to the ramming of *U-254* but, he wonders, was it entered this way, to hush up the fact that a fellow U-boat commander abandoned a U-boat that the second-in-command was able to save? Should the commander have been among the first to abandon the damaged vessel?

† The U-boats came in for a lot of criticism because they had orders not to pick up survivors. In truth they could only have done so at the expense of their operational efficiency. Every inch of space was crammed with supplies. The few bunks and hammocks on board had to be shared by watchmen. A 'hot bed' system. Food was limited and water severly rationed. There was also the question of war secrets. The cramped confines of a U-boat would have made it almost impossible for a prisoner, held there for days or weeks, not to learn all the innermost secrets of how a U-boat operated. Prisoners had been known to escape and get back to Allied lines. The only persons who could be picked, out of the water were Allied airmen shot down over the Bay of Biscay. They could rapidly be returned to a French base. The reason why they, and not seamen, were allowed to be picked up was that it was hoped that such an airman might be 'persuaded' to part with the information of how it was that our planes were finding U-boats so frequently. Doenitz desperately wanted to discover RAF secret weapons on board. There were cases throughout the war when German crews, on Captain's orders, gave water and cigarettes to lifeboats full of survivors from the ships they had sunk; although even this was probably against orders. Men of the sea respect other men of the sea: much as airmen respect brother airmen, war or no war.

B/120 and *Potentilla*) what was it that Terry Bulloch attacked and why were the seagulls flocking to feast upon something thrown up from below? And who were the dead bodies that *Potentilla* observed?

Air Combat Report to HQ 16 Group,
12 September 1940

(a) *Time, date, and position* :- 1950 hrs. 6/9/40 about 85 miles N.E. of Cromer.

(b) *Aircraft type, letter, squadron, and crew*:- Hudson W/206.
Pilot:- F/O Bulloch   Navigator:- P/O Heaphy
W/O:- Sgt. Arnott   A/G:- Sgt. Coldbeck

(c) *Narrative of first sighting*:- Hudson was cruising at 140 kts. at a height of 500 ft: sighted a Heinkel He 115 floatplane at 400 ft. on a track of 300 degrees (T). When first sighted the Heinkel was about 400 yards ahead of the Hudson just crossing its track almost at right angles.

(d) *Narrative of the approach*:- Hudson altered course to port and opened up to about 180 kts. and rapidly overhauled the E/A which was considerably slower.

(e) *Narrative of the attack*:- At a range of about 150 yards the Hudson opened fire with front guns from almost dead astern and put in three or four bursts which appeared to enter the wings and fuselage of the Heinkel. Return fire from enemy rear gunner was experienced.

The Heinkel took avoiding action by diving slightly and executing S turns.

The Hudson then pulled off and overshot to starboard of the E/A and slightly above him, and then started a wide turn to port.

As the Hudson banked the turret gunner opened up over the mainplane and followed the He 115 round, firing several short burst of 30-40 rounds each. The turret gunner states that he had difficulty in keeping the target in his sights on account of the smoke and flash from his incendiary; in fact he had to slacken fire on this account. At this time the port

K-gun was firing one complete pan in several bursts, which were seen to go slightly above and then into the E/A, at ranges between 200 and 250 yards.

Occasional return fire was experienced from the Heinkel's rear gunner at this time.

It was approaching dusk now and the Hudson lost sight of the E/A temporarily, but on turning saw him and gave chase again, making another front gun attack from dead astern and slightly above. Fire was opened at a 100 yds. range and continued in successive bursts until all front gun ammunition was expended. This attack silenced the enemy rear gun. The Hudson then broke away to port, and the starboard K-gun took up the attack firing about 60 rounds at 150 yds. range: the turret guns were also fired at this stage, when the ammunition belt on the port turret gun broke, but fire was maintained from the second turret gun, and several short bursts were seen to go in or near the E/A.

The E/A engines appeared to cut out, and after the Hudson had overshot, the floatplane made a controlled landing but swung round to starboard after touching down, leaving a thick wake of oil, which was leaking in large quantities.

The Hudson then made several tight circuits around the Heinkel at a fairly low altitude firing from port K-gun and rear gun (another member of the crew presumably having taken the place of the original gunner). Again the rear gun was silenced and by now the Hudson was out of ammunition.

The E/A then fired 2 or 3 single red Verey's lights and the Hudson made a low level bombing attack 2/250 lb. bombs from 600 ft; these both fell some distance short, but the Hudson did a dive attack and the third bomb fell about 50 yds. off the Heinkel rocking it severely.

By now it was dusk and so the Hudson broke off the engagement and continued its patrol, observing the Heinkel to have both engines stopped and a list to starboard. Severe damage must also have been caused by the large number of rounds observed to go home.

One bullet hole through wing of Hudson sustained; no other damage or casualty to crew.

(g) *Particulars of opponent's armament*:- The He 115 had one free rear gun which was used extensively. It is not confirmed that any fire was seen from nose of E/A, but he was not ever in a position to bring fire to bear. What was at first thought to be a shell burst in the nose of the Hudson has since been found to be an incendiary round which caught fire in the breech of one of the front guns.

(h) *Any other information*:- The enemy aircraft was camouflaged a dark green colour.

.... Pilot.

Group Captain – Commanding
R.A.F. Station, Bircham Newton.

Appendix D

Principal U-Boat attacks by Squadron Leader Terence Malcolm Bulloch, DSO,* DFC*

Date of Attack	Official post-war assessment	U-Boat No
16 August 1942	Severe damage	U-89
18 August 1942	Severe damage	U-653
12 October 1942	Destroyed	U-597
5 November 1942	Destroyed	U-132
8 December 1942	Destroyed	U-254
8 July 1943	Destroyed	U-514

Terry Bulloch's official score, as given by the Air Historical Branch is 4 U-boats destroyed, 2 severely damaged, and one slightly damaged (the latter probably in the attack of 3rd May 1942). This score was the highest achieved by any pilot during the war. The next highest was 2 U-boats destroyed.

APPENDIX E

Sightings and Attacks on Enemy U-Boats Oct 41-Dec 42

1941	Sighting	No	Attack	No	Duty	Assessment of attack by Admiralty
Oct. 22			51°N 17°W	1	SL89	No damage
Dec. 22	45°N 19°W	3			HS76	–
1942						
Apr. 24			47°30'N 21°W	1	Sweep	Severe shaking
May 3			47°N 16°W	1	Sweep	Slight damage
Aug. 10	55°N 21°W	1			SC94	–
Aug. 16		U89	48°02'N 22°20'W	1	OS37	Very severe damage – probably destroyed
Aug. 18		U653	41°46'N 19°40'W	1	SL118	Very severe damage
Oct. 12	57°29'N 27°49'W	1	56°50'N 28°05'W	1	ONS136	Very severe damage – probably destroyed
Oct. 16			55°45'N 26°48'W	1	SC104	No damage
Oct. 28	55°23'N 26°54'W	1	55°26'N 27°04'W	1	HX212	–
	55°27'N 26°48'W					
Nov. 5	58°30'N 32°52'W	1	58°08'N 33°18'W	1	SC107	Very severe damage – probably destroyed
			58°05'N 32°57'W	1		
Dec. 8	57°37'N 34°32'W	U254 1	57°25'N 35°19'W	1	HX217	–
			57°37'N 34°42'W	1	HX217	Confirmed Kill
			57°57'N 33°51'W	1	HX217	2 DC's only – analyses well?
			57°45'N 33°45'W	1	HX217	⎫
			57°58'N 33°38'W	1	HX217	⎬ Cannon attacks only
			57°55'N 33°36'W	1	HX217	⎪
			58°27'N 33°08'W	1	HX217	⎭

Index

Airfields:
Aldergrove, 97, 98, 119
Ayr, 120
Ballykelly, 140, 165
Beaulieu, 154, 155
Bircham Newton, 75, 78, 83, 84, 86, 90, 92, 93, 94, 95, 98
Boscombe Down, 93, 156. 157, 160, 165
Hendon, 77
Limavady, 118, 131
Lyneham, 174, 177
Mildenhall, 91
Netheravon, 71, 72, 75
Newtownards, 68
Nutts Corners, 27, 28, 29, 51, 113, 114, 115, 119. 120, 122, 132, 178, 181
Predannack, 140
Prestwick, 71, 115, 120, 133, 154, 165, 177
Reyjavik, 28, 134ff
St Eval, 130, 131, 160
Silloth, 94, 95
Squire's Gate, 112
Tain, 166, 172
Wick, 133
Arnott, Sgt, 195

Bader, Sir Douglas, 77
Berman, Shelley, 183, 184
Bernhard, Prince, 153
Bulloch, Mrs Barbara, 92
Bulloch, Mrs Elsie, 55, 56, 62
Bulloch, Larmor, 54, 56, 58, 59, 60, 61, 62, 64, 68, 92
Bulloch, Mrs Linda, 186
Bulloch, S.A.M., 54, 55, 61, 62
Bulloch, Yvonne (Mrs Y. Boyd), 54, 55, 56, 57, 59, 60, 61, 65, 68, 69, 77, 152, 180

Capper, F/O, 71
Chamberlain, Neville, 78, 90, 93
Cheshire, Gp Capt Leonard, 153
Churchill, Sir Winston, 25, 27, 69, 93, 122, 123, 133, 142
Coldbeck, Sgt, 99, 195
Cundy, F/O (later W/Cmdr) Peter, 123, 124

Dear, P/O, 125, 137
Doenitz, Grand Admiral K, 21, 24, 40, 44, 48, 50, 51, 53, 88, 97, 127, 134, 145, 148, 149, 161, 189, 193
Durrant, P/O Frank, 162

Erskine, Rev. David, 65

George VI, King, 51, 56, 131
Goodfellow, P/O, 137, 142

Harris, Air Chief Marshal Sir Arthur 'Bomber', 88
Harrison, F/Lt (later S/Lr) 'Harry John', 119, 124, 125
Heaphy, P/O, 195
Hitler, Adolph, 24, 69, 77, 78, 84, 88, 149, 176
Hollis, Sgt, 130

Isted, S/Ldr Desmond, 30, 48, 52, 150

Kretschmer, Kapitänleutnant Otto, 48, 49, 145

Layton, F/O (later F/Lt) Michael, RCAF, 31, 32, 33, 35, 50, 52, 142, 144, 152, 153, 168
Le Brun, French President, 80
Leigh, W/C, de Vere 156
Lewis, F/Lt A.D. 'Sandy', 159, 160, 164
Lord, Sgt (later P/O), 162, 168, 169, 170, 173

McBratney, W/C (later G/Cpt) V.H.A., 27, 124, 133, 134, 186
McColl, Sgt (later F/Lt) R.J. 'Jock', 32, 34, 35, 36, 42, 52, 125, 126, 131, 138, 142, 144, 152, 156, 159, 160, 162, 167, 168, 169, 171, 175, 178, 182, 185, 190
McTaggart-Cowen, 110
McIntyre, S/Ldr David, 71
Mitchell, P/O, 125, 137
Mitchell, Capt (later General) 'Billy', USAAF, 81
Mussolini, Benito, 69, 77

Neville, P/O, 137

Page, Capt (BOAC), 120
Patrick, S/Ldr, 178
Patterson, F/O (later S/Ldr) Ian, 103, 105, 107, 111, 112, 113, 118
Peck, Col Walter D.. (USAAF), 106, 107, 108
Percy, Capt Jim, (BOAC), 117
Perioli, F/O, 72
Peyton Ward, Capt D.V. (RN), 189-195
Poland, Lt (R.N.), 97
Pound, Admiral of the Fleet Sir Dudley, 25, 27, 122

Roosevelt, President Franklin Delano, 27, 104, 108, 123
Roskill, Capt Stephen, (R.N.), 189-194
Ross, Donald, 103, 105, 107, 110, 113, 120

Schendel, Kapitänleutnant, 170
Ships:
  Allied
  Ark Royal HMS, 89, 122
  Barham HMS, 113
  Bazeley, HMS, 170
  Bentinck, HMS, 170
  Burza (Polish), 49
  Courageous HMS, 89, 122
  Drury HMS, 170
  Eglantine (Norwegian), 49
  Flame HMS, 49
  Formidable HMS, 112
  Glorious HMS, 122

Letitia SS, 139
Leopoldville (Troopship), 102, 103, 116
Nelson HMS, 81, 151
Orissa HMS, 136
Potentilla (Norwegian), 38, 39, 40, 49, 190-194
Rose (Norwegian), 49
Royal Oak, HMS, 89
Royal Sovereign, HMS, 103
H-32 HM Submarine, 157
Tetela SS, 116
Vervian HMS, 49
German
Bismarck, 12, 149
Gneisenau, 83, 131
Prinz Eugen, 131
Scharnhorst, 131
Tirpitz, 131
U-89, 140, 199
U-132 146, 147, 199
U-221, 188, 190, 191,
U-254, 39, 190-195, 199
U-410, 188
U-514, 161, 174, 199
U-570, 134
U-597, 143, 145, 146, 199
U-636, 167, 170, 171, 174
U-653, 141, 199
Smith, Howard, 57, 59
Squadrons:
  53: 14
  59: 123, 165, 172
  86: 132, 166, 172, 174
  120: 17, 27, 28, 45, 50, 51, 113, 114, 119, 120, 122-50, 151, 157, 180, 186, 190-191, 199
  206: 93-101, 109, 130, 131, 195
  220: 75, 78, 80, 81, 82, 84, 85-92, 93
  221: 118
  224: 159-164, 173, 188
  231: 177
  311: 164
  500: 112, 124
  504: 124

Thomas, Sir Miles, 133
Thomson, P/O, RCAF, 32, 142
Tizard, Sir Henry, 132
Turner, F/Sgt, G.W. 'Ginger' Turner

(RAF), 31, 32, 33, 52, 125, 126, 131, 135, 138, 142, 144, 152

Vickers, S/Ldr (later W/C) Tim, 90

Watson, F/O Willie, 109
Walton, F/O R., 123
Wightman, F/O Richard, 123
Winn, Commander R, (RNVR), 136
Winston, F/E John (BOAC), 182, 183